I0479435

# BEGINNING WITH
# Q-BASIC

## POORNIMA GONTIYA

INDEPENDENTLY PUBLISHED

Copyright © 2023 POORNIMA GONTIYA

All rights reserved

The characters and events portrayed in this book are fictitious. Any similarity to real persons, living or dead, is coincidental and not intended by the author.

No part of this book may be reproduced, or stored in a retrieval system, or transmitted in any form or by any means, electronic, mechanical, photocopying, recording, or otherwise, without express written permission of the publisher.

ISBN-13: 9798389720435
ISBN-10: 1477123456

Cover design by: Art Painter
Library of Congress Control Number: 2018675309
Printed in the United States of America

This book is dedicated to my teacher, my mentor, guide and philosopher who has nourished me with her blessings and immense knowledge.

Dr. Samridhi Paranjpey (ma'am)

*"A HAPPY HEART AND A SMILING FACE ARE THE COMPLEMENTRY, YOU SMILE WHEN YOU ARE HAPPY AND YOU BECOME HAPPY WHEN YOU SMILE*
*SO KEEP SMILING"*

*- Dr. SAMRIDHI PARANJPEY (ma'am)*

# INTRODUCTION

This book is the bridge to connect the basic and advance knowledge of q basic.

The complexity of the programming language of q basic has been simplified for the better understanding of the students and the beginners who want to learn from the basic till advance level.

During the making of this book many challenges has been dealt regarding the understanding of the complex programs and using them in the q basic application for debugging process.

The algorithms and implementation of the program has been made user-friendly and specially it has been modified in the way which students can learn to use it easily.

This book will be the path finder for the students who are facing problems regarding the simple programming.

I hope that this book will be the most useful book for everyone who are interested to learn the q basic language.

# TABLE OF CONTENTS

<u>VARIABLE -</u>

<u>NUMERICALS -</u>

<u>1. STRING/ ALPHA NUMERIC/NON-NUMERIC</u>

**2. numeric -**

*SYMBOLS AND ITS USE*

**Flowcharts**

**The Basic Symbols of a Flowchart**

**What is a Flowchart?**

**Flowchart Symbols**

**How to Make a Flowchart**

**Types and Uses of Flowcharts**

<u>**Flowcharts**</u>

❖ <u>Project planning</u>

❖ <u>Program or system design through flowchart programming</u>

❖ <u>Process documentation</u>

❖ <u>Audit a process for inefficiencies or malfunctions</u>

❖ <u>Map computer algorithms</u>

❖ <u>Documenting workflow</u>

**1. KEYWORD**

**2. Character Set**

**3.Variables**

**Rules for naming a variable**

**4. Constants**

**5. Operator and Operands**

*Operators*

**c. Logical Operators**

**6. Expression**

**7. Statements**

**PROGRAMMING**

**CLS Statement**

**REM .**

# INTRODUCTION TO QBASIC

It was intended as a replacement for GW-BASIC. QBasic was based on earlier Quick BASIC 4.5 compiler. It does not produce .exe files but instead generates files with extension .bas which can only be executed immediately by the built in QBasic interpreter. It is based on DOS operating systems but is also executable on windows.

Q Basic is a structured programming language, supporting constructs such as subroutines. Line numbers, a concept often associated with BASIC, are supported for compatibility, but are not considered good form, having been replaced by descriptive line labels.

QBasic has limited support for user-defined data types (structures), and several primitive types used to contain strings of text or numeric data. It supports various inbuilt functions.

For its time, QBasic provided a state-of-the-art IDE, including a debugger with features such as on-the-fly expression evaluation and code modification .

**[QBasic is an integrated development environment and interpreter for a variety of dialects of BASIC which are based on QuickBasic. Code entered into the IDE is compiled to an intermediate representation, and this IR is immediately executed on demand within the IDE. ]**

QBASIC is a high level programming language that allows

us to write programs. BASIC uses English like words and mathematical symbols to write programs. The programs written in QBASIC need to be converted into machine codes. QBASIC provides working area to write programs and QBASIC has its own Interpreter.

QBASIC converts one statement of a program into machine code at a time. After the execution of the previous statement, it converts another statement of the program into machine code and so on. For this reason, QBASIC is also called an Interpreter.

QBASIC Editor checks syntax errors and capitalizes QBASIC reversed words. QBASIC Editor provides all the facilities that are required for programs. In the QBASIC Editor; you can write, edit, run and debug programs.

The functions of Q-basic are the readymade programs that take some data, manipulate them and return the value, which may be a string or numeric type. Programming languages also have certain functions like spreadsheets or database software.

## FEATURE OF QBASIC

Some features of QBASIC are listed below:-

a. It does not use technical terminology (word) to write statements.
b. It automatically checks syntax.
c. It capitalizes the reserved words.
d. It keeps the same variable name used in a program to identical form.
e. It allows you to break lengthy programs into modules.
f. It interprets a statement of a program at a time to CPU.
g. It is a compiler-based language.
h. It does not require specifying line numbers.

i. It works with numeric as well as non-numeric data.

j. It is useful for mathematical, scientific and engineering purposes as well.

## Loading Qbasic

QBASIC programming language consists of two files: QBASIC.EXE and QBASIC.HLP. Normally these files are found in a folder named 'QBASIC' which is in drive C

To start QBASIC, follow these steps.

- Click the Start button.
- Point to All Programs and then Accessories.
- Select Command Prompt. It displays Command Prompt Window.
- To move to the root directory, at DOS prompt, type CD\ and press Enter key.
- At C:\> prompt, type CD QBASIC and press Enter key.
- At C:\ QBASIC> prompt, type q-basic and press Enter key. It will display QBASIC Welcome Screen.
- Press Esc key to get QBASIC Editor Screen.

## Q-Basic Editor Screen

## Q`Basic Editor Is The Window Where You Write Programs. The Editor Provides All The Facilities To Write Programs And Editing Them.

## Q-Basic Editor Screen Has Four Parts.
## A. Menu Bar.

# B. Program Window
# C. Immediate Window
# D. Status Bar

### a. Menu Bar

The Menu Bar consists of list of commands like File, View, Search, Run, Debug, Options and Help. These menus again have some sub commands such as FILE= New, Open, Save, Save As, Print, Exit. EDIT= Cut, Copy, Paste, Clear, New Sub, New Function. VIEW= Subs, Spilt, Output Screen. SEARCH= Find, Repeat Last Find, Change. RUN= Start, Restart, Continue. DEBUG= Step, Procedure Step, Trace On, Toggle Breakpoint, Clear All Breakpoints break points , Set Next Statement. OPTIONS= Display, Help Path, Syntax Checking.

### b. Program Window

The upper window which is titled as 'Untitled' is the window where you write programs. This window is called Program Window. To see the output of the statements written in this window, you need to press Shift + F5 key.

### c. Immediate Window

The lower window which is titled as 'Immediate' is known as Immediate Window where you test commands, expressions etc. As soon as you press Enter key, it displays the output on the screen.
Note: F6 function key is used to switch from Program Window to Immediate Window and vice versa.

### d. Status Bar

The status bar shows short cut keys and the location of the cursor on the screen.

## RUNNING A PROGRAM

After entering a set of instructions in the Program Window, you may want to see the output of the program. To see the output of the program you need to run a program. When you run a program QBASIC converts and directs each statement of a program at a time to the CPU. To run (execute) a program

Press Shift + F5 key or press Alt, R, S.

*Note\*\**
*F5 key is used for continuing the program from the previous stop statement.*

## SAVING A PROGRAM

You need to save a program for the future use. Sometimes you need to save incomplete program so that you can complete at next time.

**To save a program, follow these steps:**

Press ALT + F key.

Highlight Save As Option.

Press Enter key. It displays Save Dialog Box.

Enter Filename in the Filename text box.

Press Enter key.

Note:\*\*\*When you supply filename just use not more than eight characters for filename.

*QBASIC automatically adds an extension as .BAS for the program file.*

# Clearing Program Window

To write a new program you need to remove the previous program from the Program Window. To clear or remove the previous program, follow these steps.
a) Press ALT key.
b) Highlight New option and press Enter key. OR. Press F, N keys.

# Opening An Existing Program

To open an existing program in the Program Window, follow these steps.
a. Press Alt key.
b. Press F key.
c. Highlight Open command and press Enter key.
d. Select a program file the list of files displayed in the Open Dialog box and press Enter key.

### EXITING QBASIC

To exit from the QBASIC, follow these steps.
a. Press ALT key. It will activate menu.
b. Press F or Enter key.
c. Press X or select Exit command under File menu and press Enter key.

# Formula Of Qbasic

In QBasic an equation has a basic setup a right side and a left side.
For instance
$X=2$,

as you can probably figure out, this sets the variable X to 2. But we can use variables on the right side too.

**Y=X*10**

would set Y equal to 10 times X, in this situation, 20 .

## How To Open And Run Qbasic

Click the Start button to display the Start menu. Point to Programs. Choose MS-DOS Prompt and an MS-DOS Prompt window opens. **At the C:\> prompt (or at the C:\Windows> prompt), type QBASIC and press the ENTER key** and the QBASIC editor appears.

the above screen is the welcome screen of QBASIC if you have already installed it in your pc for removing this window you can just press the Esc button. Now let's move to the next step of using the q basic .

## Steps For Writing A Program In Qbasic

*STEP 1* *from keyboard type your program on your computer screen*

example

PRINT "welcome to this world"

END

*STEP 2  If you type "print" in lower case, the QBasic system will automatically change it to upper case.*

If you make mistakes, use the arrow keys on the keyboard to move the cursor (the yellow underscore) to the mistake. Use the delete (Del) key or the backspace key to remove the mistake and enter the correct characters.

If the system is not accepting the characters you have typed or starts showing menus you don't want) hit the **Escape** key to come out of that screen.

*STEP 3*

click on RUN option using your mouse . the dropdown menu will appear click on start or you can also Run the program by tapping the F5 key (on the top row of the keyboard). The program starts executing statements one by one starting with the first statement. This program prints "welcome to this world" to the screen:

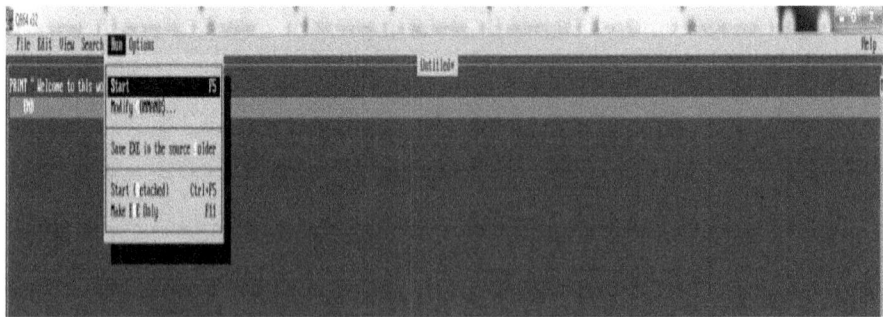

the output will come like this ↓

congratulations you have successfully run your first program.

## STEP 4 How to Save a Program to a Source File

A "source file" is a permanent disk file that contains a program. Unless you save your program to a file, it will be lost forever when you leave or end the QBasic from your system. With a short program, this might not matter. But if you are creating an assignment or program with some important statements you should save it to the disk before leaving from that page.

for saving your project you can also go to file on the dropdown menu go to save

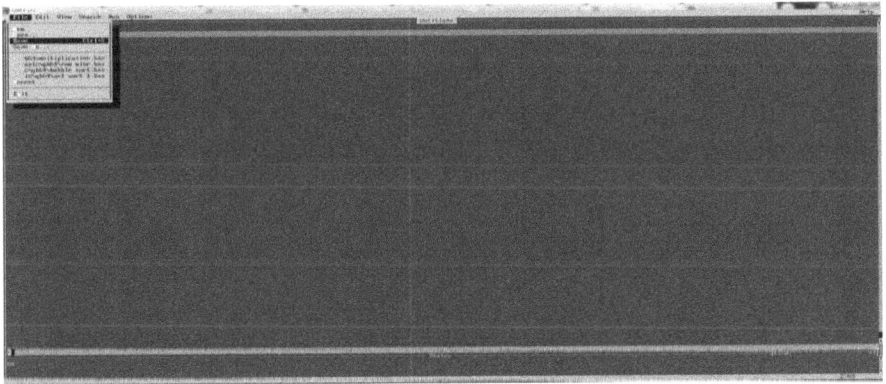

\*\*\*\*\*\*\*\*\*\*\*\*\*\*\*\*\*\*\*\*\*\*\*\*\*\*\*\*\*\*\*\*\*\*\*\*\*\*\*\*\*\*\*\*\*\*\*\*\*\*\*\*\*\*\*\*\*\*\*\*\*\*\*\*\*\*\*\*\*\*\*\*\*\*\*\*\*\*\*\*\*\*\*

note\*\*

as soon as you leave that page the window will popup saying you have not saved your project yet. on that popup window go to save and hit enter button or just click on it.

as soon as you click on save option you will be directed to this popup window.

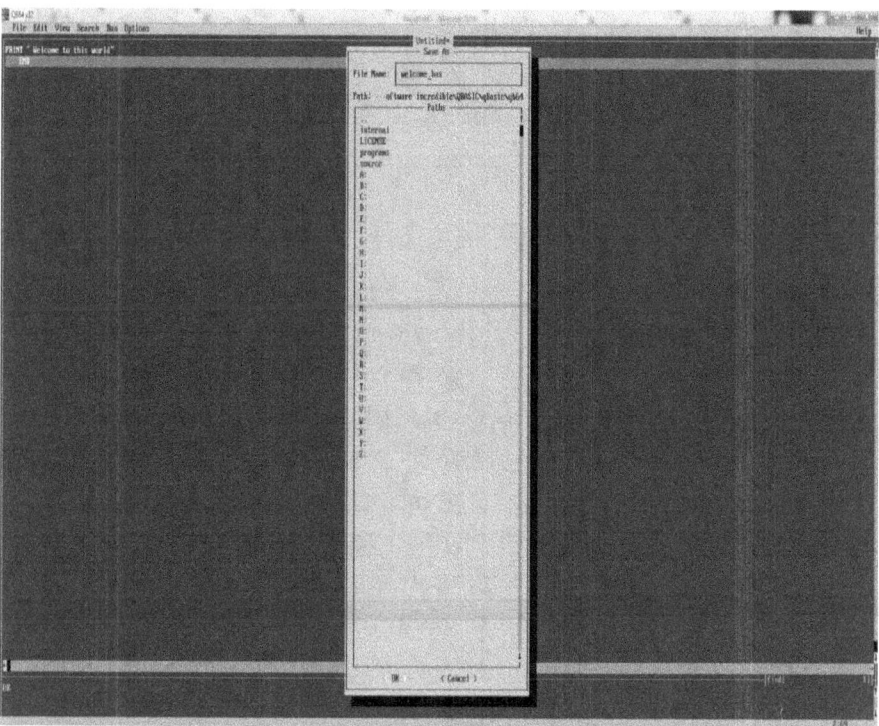

write the desired name on the untitled name and save it by clicking on ok .

## STEP 5 How to Load a Program from a Disk File

You can load QBasic with a program that has been saved as a disk file.

click on file then go to open and find the name of your saved file then click on it .

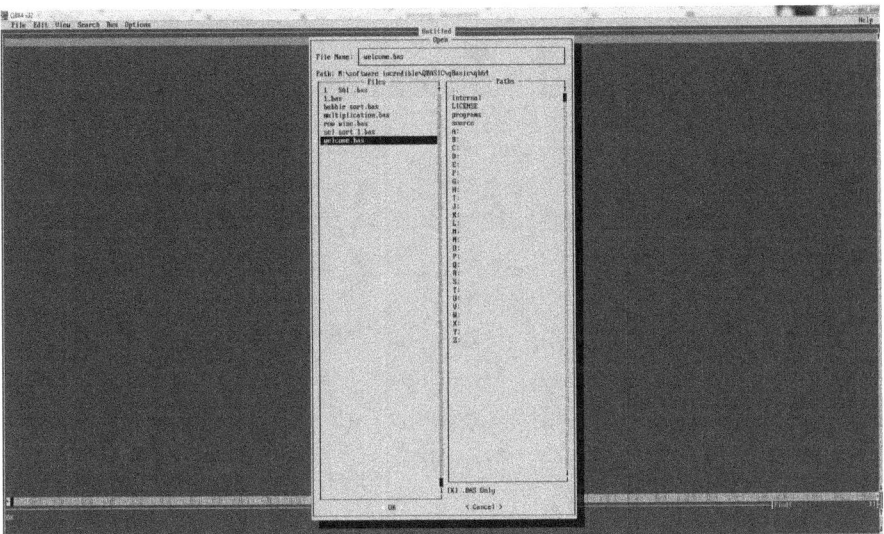

**click OK**

# Deleting The Program (To Erase The Current Program):

> ➢ Go to the "File" menu.
> ➢ Click "New."
> ➢ The interpreter asks if you want to save the program.
> ➢ Select "No" (or if you'd rather keep the program, select "Yes").

# Important Terms Used In Qbasic

*Programs, commands, strings, expressions, languages, assembly language, compiler,*

*Interpretater , flowcharting, variables, symbols, rem , input, if statement*

*Goto statement , looping statement, while, wend*

# Some Basic Useful Commands On Qbasic:

### 1. PRINT:

This command prints the statement or data written after it. If the data to be printed is a string then it is written inside double quotes (" ") and if it is a number or a variable it can be written directly.

### Example:

PRINT "WELCOME TO THIS WORLD"

PRINT WELCOME TO THIS WORLD

### 2. INPUT:

INPUT command is used to take inputs/data from the user. It can be used to input both strings and numbers.

If the data to be taken is a numerical value then the variable name in which it is to be stored is written directly after the INPUT command.

### Syntax:

INPUT "[message to user]"; [variable_name]

### Example:

INPUT age

If the data to be taken is string then the variable name in which it is to be stored is written followed by $ after the INPUT command.

INPUT name$

## 3. CLS:

CLS stands for Clear Screen and is used to clear the screen, if some previous results/outputs are still present on the screen. Below is a simple program to illustrate above commands:

Output:

# Explanation:

When using INPUT commands, users are presented with the message associated with it and are asked to input values to variables.
PRINT statement prints the statements associated with it.

# Applications Of Q-Basic:

❖ QBasic is the most suitable language for the beginners to start with. It introduces people to programming without any need to worry about the internal working of the computer.

❖ QBasic is very easy and simple to apply and create

business applications, for creating games and even simple databases. It offers commands like SET, CIRCLE, LINE, etc which allow the programmer to draw using Q-basic. Hence, graphics can also be created using QBasic.

❖ QBasic also supports creating sounds of some desired frequency through the speakers of your PC. Though only one sound can be played at once.

# Advantages Of Qbasic:

❖ The key feature of the language is its close resemblance to English.
❖ Syntax of your code is checked automatically.
❖ Q-basic has a dynamic program debugging feature.
❖ Lengthy programs can be broken into smaller modules

# Disadvantages Of Qbasic:

❖ The language is not structured.
❖ Q-basic is DOS based and has now become obsolete and is limited only in the field of education and programming.

△△△

# OPERATOR IN QBASIC

Operators are the foundation of any programming language . They are the certain symbols which tells the computer to perform certain calculations such as mathematical and logical calculation. We can also define operators as symbols that help us to perform specific mathematical and logical computations on operands. In other words, we can say that an operator operates the operands. For example, '+' is an operator used for addition, '-' for subtraction and so on . as shown below are the examples of addition and subtraction .

c = a + b ; c = a - b

Here, '+' is the operator known as the addition operator , '-' is the subtraction operator and 'a' and 'b' are operands. The addition operator tells the compiler to add and subtract both of the operands 'a' and 'b'.

The functionality of the Q-Basic programming is incomplete without the use of these operators.

Types of operators in Q-Basic are :-

1. Mathematical Operators

2. Relational Operators

3. Logical Operators

## Mathematical Operators

QBASIC can perform the following arithmetic expression involving the five arithmetic operators such as :

*+ (addition), - (subtraction), \* (multiplication, / (division) and ^*
*(exponentiation).*

| Operator | function | Example | Result |
|----------|----------|---------|--------|
| + | Add | 2 + 2 | 4 |
| - | Subtract | 5 - 2 | 3 |
| * | Multiply | 7 * 3 | 21 |
| / | Divide | 8 / 2 | 4 |

Arithmetical operators are used to perform mathematical calculations in a program. These operators work in the same sequence in which they are used in mathematics ( i.e., BODMAS).

Example 1:

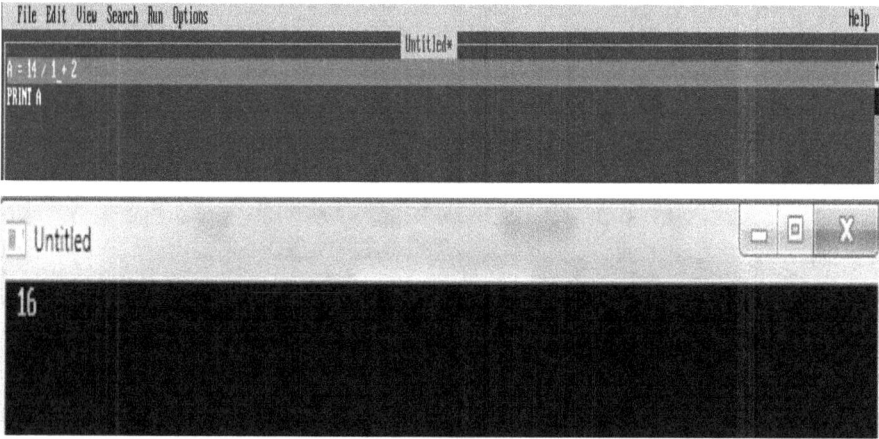

Example2:

```
 File  Edit  View  Search  Run  Options                                    Help
                              Untitled*
PRINT "Enter the first number"
INPUT a
PRINT "Enter the second number"
INPUT b
c = a + b
d = a * b
PRINT a; "+"; b; "="; c
PRINT a; "*"; b; "="; d
END
```

OUTPUT

```
Untitled
Enter the first number
? 2
Enter the second number
? 4
2 + 4 = 6
2 * 4 = 8
```

# Advanced Operations:

| Operator | What it does | Example | Result |
|---|---|---|---|
| \ | divides and turns the result into an integer(the whole number) | 21 \ 7 | 3 |
| ^ | Raises a number to the power of another number | 2 ^ 4 (means: 2*2*2*2) 1.5 ^ 3 (means:1.5*1.5*1.5) | 16 3.375 |
| SQR | Calculates the square root of a number | SQR(9) SQR(16) SQR(5) | 3(because:3^2=9) 4 (because:4^2=16) 2.236 |
| MOD | Divides two numbers, and if the result is not an integer (for example - 3.25), finds out how much to subtract from the first number in order to get the integer result. | 17 MOD 5 | 2(because:17 / 5 = 3.4 17 – 2 = 15 15 / 5 = 3) |

*The hierarchy of operations is as follows:*

- Exponential
- Multiplication and division
- Addition and subtraction

*In addition to this hierarchy of operations, the following rules must be kept in mind in arithmetic expression:*

- Two operations must not appear together. For example, C+-D, A/-C, etc are not permitted.
- String constants and string variables should not be used in arithmetic expressions. For example ., P+P$ is wrong.
- When brackets are used, they must be used in pairs, i.e. every left bracket must be matched with a right bracket.
- Denominator of an expression should not be zero.
- Within a given pair of parentheses, the natural hierarchy of operations will apply.

- Let us take an example where we give QBASIC equivalents of a few algebraic expressions.

| Algebraic Expression | QBASIC Equivalent |
|---|---|
| -2A+B | -2*A+B |
| -A+B/C+D | -(A+B)/(C+D) |
| -A(B+C) | -A*(B+C) |
| -B2-4AC | -B^2-4*A*C |

```
1 CLS 'this command clears the screen, so it's empty
INPUT "Enter the first number "; a
INPUT "Enter the second number "; b
IF b = 0 THEN 'checks if the second number is zero,
   'because you can't divide by zero
   PRINT "the second number cannot be 0. Try again."
   DO: LOOP WHILE INKEY$ = "" 'waits for you to press a key to continue
   GOTO 1 'then sends you back to line 1
END IF
CLS 'clear the screen again
c = a MOD b
d = a / b
e = a - c
f = e / b
PRINT a; "MOD"; b; "="; c
IF c = 0 THEN 'this checks if the result of a MOD b = 0, because
   'it means that the result of a / b is integer
   PRINT "because"; a; "/"; b; "="; d; " - integer. Try again."
   DO: LOOP WHILE INKEY$ = "" 'waits for you to press a key to continue
   GOTO 1 'then sends you back to the line 1
END IF
PRINT "because"; a; "/"; b; "="; d; " -not integer" 'The rest of the program
PRINT "but"; a; "-"; c; "="; e 'executes if the result of
PRINT "and"; e; "/"; b; "="; f; " - integer" 'a / b is not integer
END
```

OUTPUT

```
Enter the first number ? _
```

```
Enter the first number ? 4
Enter the second number ? 6
```

```
4 MOD 6 = 4
because 4 / 6 = .6666667  -not integer
but 4 - 4 = 0
and 0 / 6 = 0  - integer
```

## 2. Relational Operator :- A relational operator is used to determine the relationship between two or more operands. The

23

relational operator checks the conditions and returns the result in either 'true' or 'false' for further processing. Examples: less than, greater than, equal, Not equal.

| Operator Meaning Example | Meaning | Example |
|---|---|---|
| < | less than | 2<5 |
| > | greater than | 5>3 |
| <= | less than or equal to | 2<=3 |
| >= | greater than or equal to | 3>=3 |
| = | equal to | 2=2 |
| <> | not equal to | 3 <> 2 |

## Logical Operators:- Logical operators are to perform logical operations on numerical values. Logical operators are used to connect two or more relations and return a TRUE or FALSE value to be used in a decision.

The common logical operators are:

- AND Conjunction
- OR Disjunction
- NOT Logical Negation

| Operator | Meaning | Example |
|---|---|---|
| **AND** | Logical AND | A>5 AND B>15 |
| **OR** | Logical OR | A>5 OR B>15 |
| **NOT** | Logical NOT | A>5 NOT B>15 |

For example, the expression A>5 AND B>15 is TRUE when A is more than 5 and at the same time B is more than 15 . Logical operators return results as indicated in the following tables. T indicates a TRUE and F indicates FALSE. X and Y are relational expressions.

**AND Operator**

| X | Y | X && Y |
|---|---|---|
| TRUE | FALSE | FALSE |
| FALSE | TRUE | FALSE |
| TRUE | TRUE | TRUE |
| FALSE | FALSE | FALSE |

## OR Operator

| X | Y | X \|\| Y |
|---|---|---|
| TRUE | FALSE | TRUE |
| FALSE | TRUE | TRUE |
| TRUE | TRUE | TRUE |
| FALSE | FALSE | FALSE |

# NOT Operator

| X ! X | Y ! X |
|---|---|
| T | F |
| F | T |

## exercise

1. Display the output of the following QBASIC program:

```
CLS
C = 3
D = C*2
START:
PRINT C,D
C = C + 2
IF C <=10 THEN GOTO START:
END
```

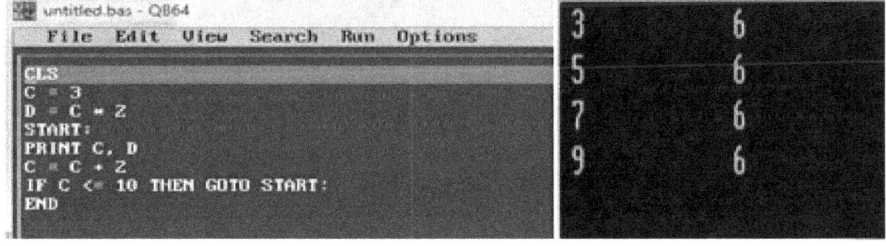

2. Display the output of the following QBASIC program:

```
CLS
P = 2
```

```
Q = 1
START :
PRINT P,Q
Q = P*Q
IF Q<=10 THEN GOTO START :
END
```

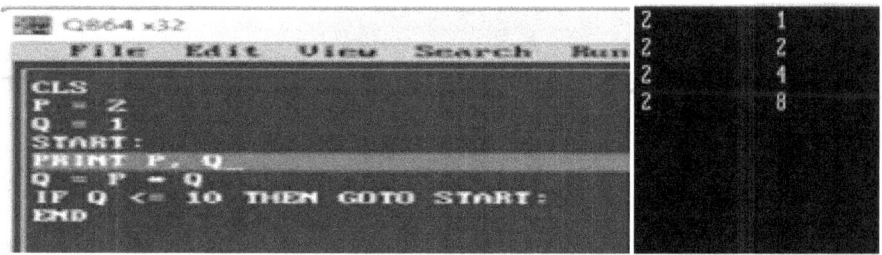

**3. Display the output of the following QBASIC program:**
```
CLS
A = 5
B = 10
START:
C = A + B
PRINT C
A = A + 1
IF A <=10 THEN GOTO START:
END
```

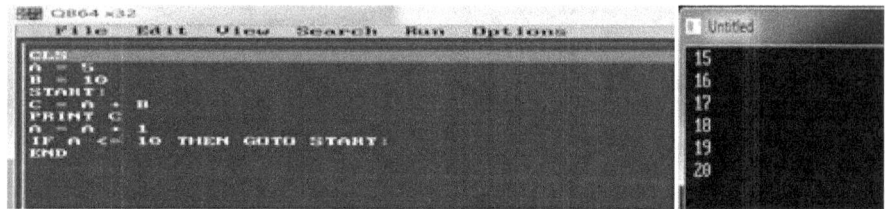

**4. Display the output of the following QBASIC program:**
```
CLS
P = 5
START:
PRINT P
P = P + 5
IF P <= 50 THEN GOTO START:
```

END

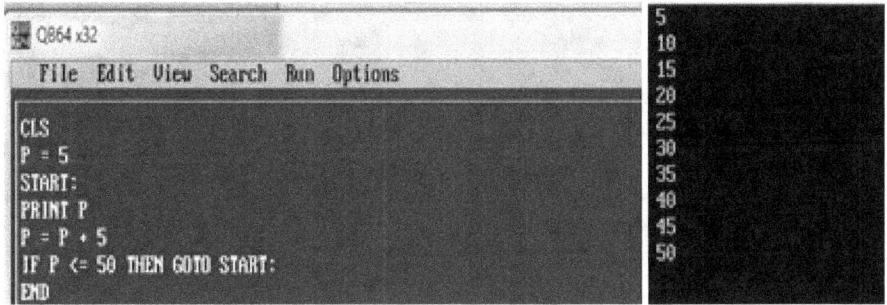

**5. Display the output of the following QBASIC program:**

CLS
A = 5
B = 10
START:
C = A + B
PRINT C
A = A + 1
IF A <=10 THEN GOTO START:
END

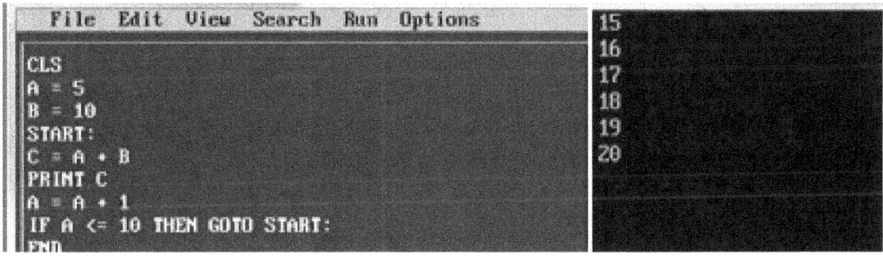

6. Display the output of the following QBASIC program:

CLS
P = 5
START:
PRINT P
P = P + 5
IF P <= 50 THEN GOTO START:
END

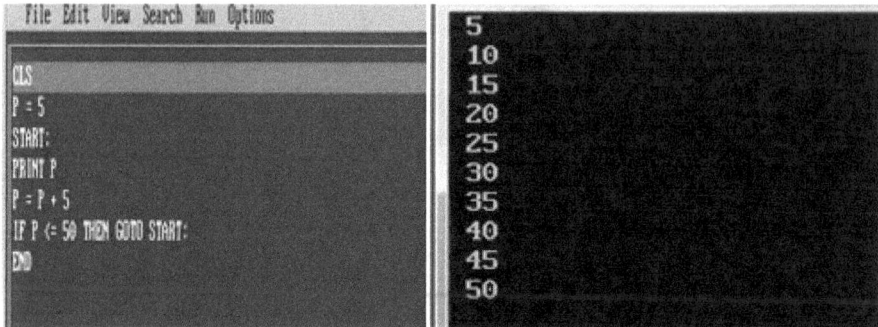

## 7. Display the output of the following QBASIC program:

```
CLS
P = 2
Q = 1
START:
PRINT P*Q
Q = Q + 1
IF Q <=10 THEN GOTO START:
END
```

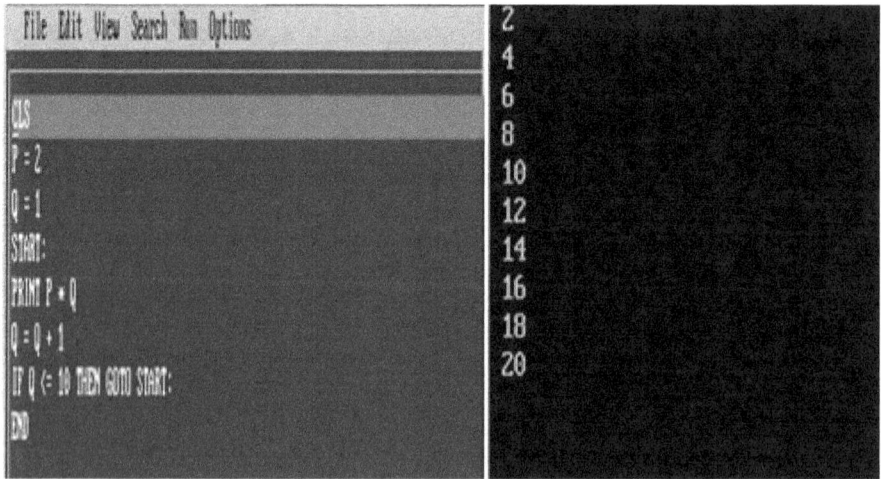

# 8. Display The Output Of The Following Qbasic Program:

**CLS**
**C = 3**
**D = C*2**
**START:**
**PRINT C,D**
**C = C + 2**
**IF C <=10 THEN GOTO START:**
**END**

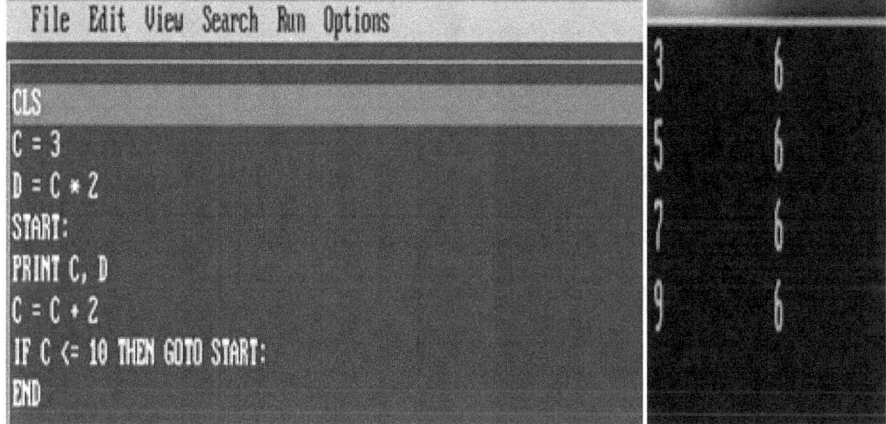

△△△

29

# BASIC FUNDAMENTALS OF Q-BASIC

**PROGRAMS - pre-stored set of instructions given in a logical sequence is called program .**

## Language

Here we have two types of language
high level ie., human language and low level ie., binary language.

ASSEMBLY LANGUAGE -

it is between machine and low level language( it is directly convertible)

COMPILER -

it converts high level program into low level program
                (It converts whole program in the
low level then execute the program).

INTERPRETATOR - it do not form object program . It interpret directly.

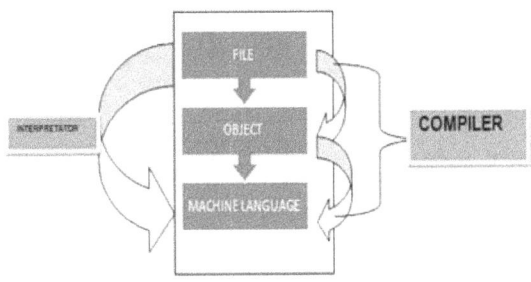

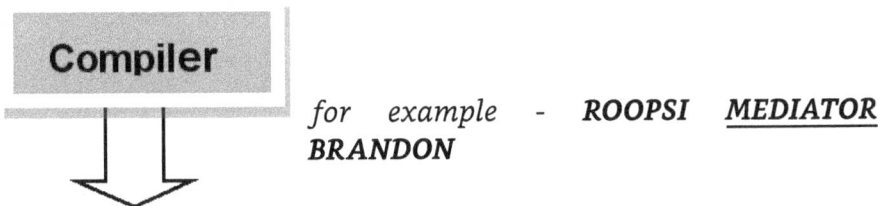

*for example* - ***ROOPSI*** ***MEDIATOR*** ***BRANDON***

Here **Roopsi** is a Hindi speaking person and only understands Hindi where as Brandon only understands English .

So here the mediator means the third person knowing both the languages works as an interpretation for both of them and translate the language vice-versa to make them understand. Given below are some of the basic fundamentals of Q-Basic which are necessary for the formation of any program and taking out it's result.

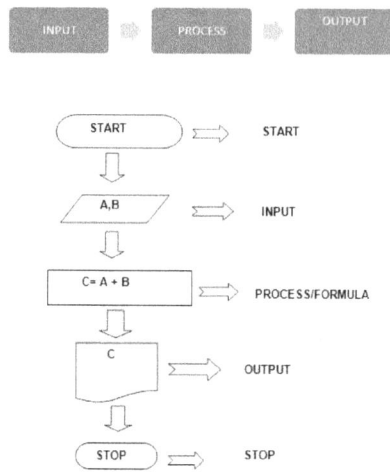

## FLOW CHARTING - ( INDEPENDENT OF ANY LANGUAGE)

❖ PRE-PLANNING OF ANY PROGRAM
❖ PICTORIAL REPRESENTATION OF ANY   PROGRAM
❖ USE - PLANNING AND DOCUMENTATION
❖ PROGRAM IS ALL ABOUT PROCESSING WHICH GETS SOMETHING AND GIVES SOMETHING.

# Variable -

variables are some symbols which represent some values.

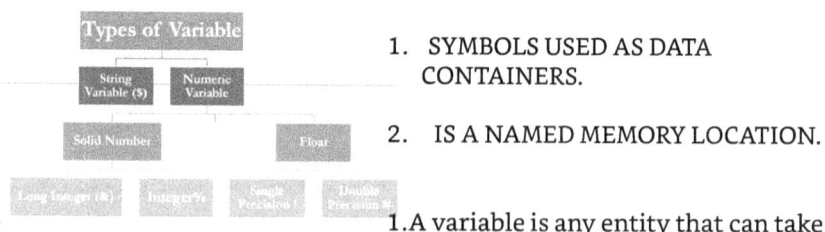

1.  SYMBOLS USED AS DATA CONTAINERS.

2.  IS A NAMED MEMORY LOCATION.

1.A variable is any entity that can take on different values. OK, so what does that mean? Anything that can vary can be considered a variable. For instance, age can be considered a variable because age can take different values for different people or for the same person at different times.

2. A variable is any characteristic, number, or quantity that can be measured or counted. A variable may also be called a data item. Age, sex, business income and expenses, country of birth, capital expenditure, class grades, eye colour and vehicle type are examples of variables.

MEMORIES HAS TWO PROPERTIES

STRING VALUE
• Strings are used for storing text/characters. For example, "hello world" is a string of characters.

NUMERIC VALUE
• A numeric value contains only numbers, a sign (leading or trailing), and a single decimal point.

3. A variable is a characteristic that can be measured and that can assume different values. Height, age, income, province or country of birth, grades obtained at school and type of housing are all examples of variables. Variables may be classified into two main categories: categorical and numeric.

# Memories Has Two Properties

string value - Strings are used for storing text/characters. For example, "hello world" is a string of characters.

numerical value - A numeric value contains only numbers, a sign (leading or trailing), and a single decimal point.

NUMERICALS - 1. STRING/ ALPHA NUMERIC/NON-NUMERIC

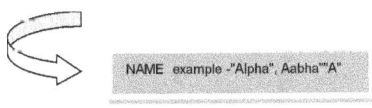

NAME example -"Alpha", Aabha""A"

2. numeric -

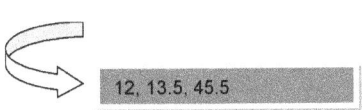

12, 13.5, 45.5

NOTE** _normalized formula will be used always. example -_

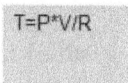

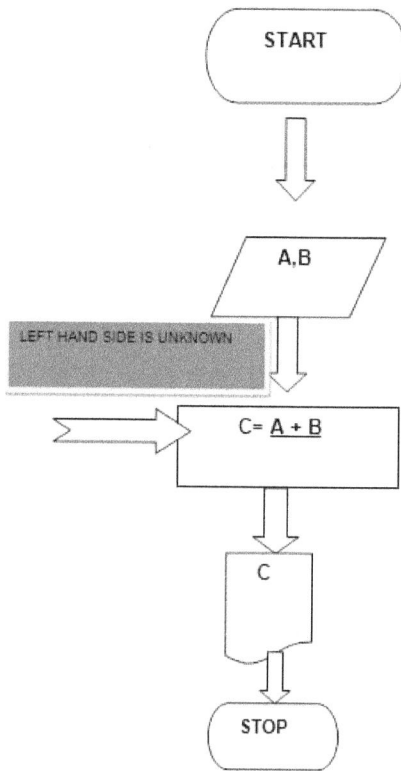

# Symbols And Its Use

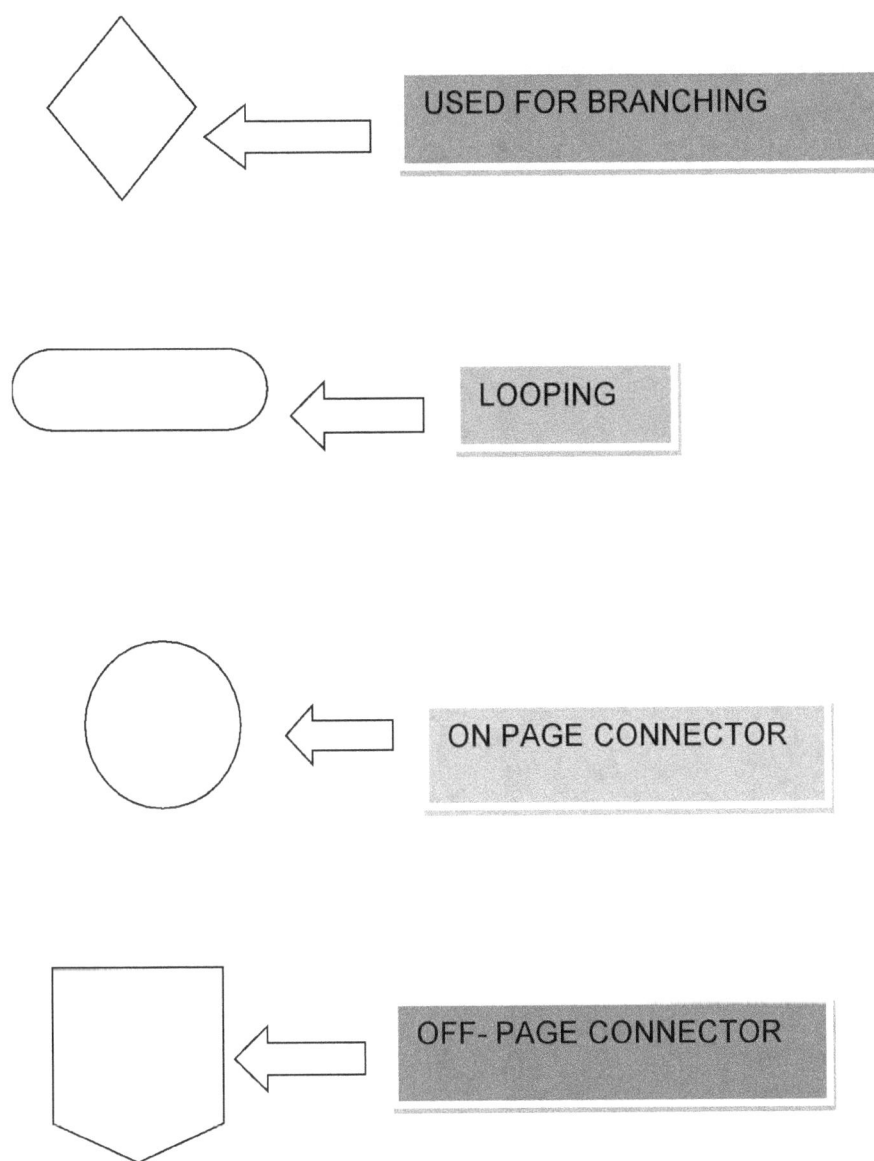

# Flowcharts

Uses special shapes to represent different types of actions or steps in a process. Lines and arrows show the sequence of the steps, and the relationships among them. These are known as flowchart symbols.

◆ **RECTANGLE SHAPE - REPRESENTS A PROCESS**
◆ **OVAL OR PILL SHAPE - REPRESENTS THE START OR END**
◆ **DIAMOND SHAPE - REPRESENTS A DECISION**
◆ **PARALLELOGRAM - REPRESENTS INPUT/OUTPUT**

| Symbol | Name | Function |
|---|---|---|
|  | Start/end | An oval represents a start or end point |
|  | Arrows | A line is a connector that shows relationships between the representative shapes |
|  | Input/Output | A parallelogram represents input or output |
|  | Process | A rectagle represents a process |
|  | Decision | A diamond indicates a decision |

# The Basic Symbols Of A Flowchart

## Start/End Symbol

The terminator symbol marks the starting or ending point of the system. It usually contains the word "Start" or "End."

## Action or Process Symbol

A box can represent a single step ("add two cups of flour"), or an entire sub-process ("make bread") within a larger process.

# Document Symbol

printed document or report.

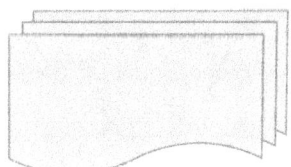

## Multiple Documents Symbol

Represents multiple documents in the process

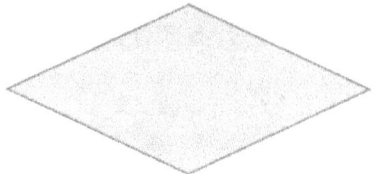

## Decision Symbol

A decision or branching point. Lines representing different decisions emerge from different points of the diamond.

## Input/output Symbol

Represents material or information entering or leaving the system, such as customer order (input) or a product (output).

## Manual Input Symbol

Represents a step where a user is prompted to enter information manually.

# Preparation Symbol

Represents a set-up to another step in the process.

## Connector Symbol

Indicates that the flow continues where a matching symbol (containing the same letter) has been placed.

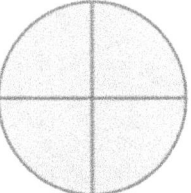

## Or Symbol

Indicates that the process flow continues in more than two branches.

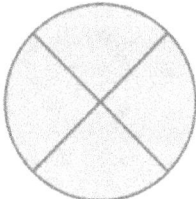

## Summoning Junction Symbol

Indicates a point in the flowchart where multiple branches converge back into a single process.

## Merge Symbol

Indicates a step where two or more sub-lists or sub-processes become one.

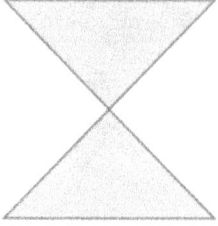

## Collate Symbol

Indicates a step that orders information into a standard format.

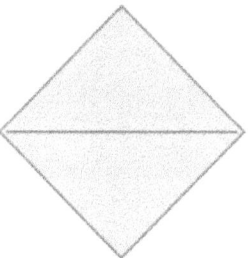

## Sort Symbol

Indicates a step that organizes a list of items into a sequence or sets based on some pre-determined criteria.

## Subroutine Symbol

Indicates a sequence of actions that perform a specific task embedded within a larger process. This sequence of actions could be described in more detail on a separate flowchart.

## Manual Loop Symbol

Indicates a sequence of commands that will continue
to repeat until stopped manually.

## Loop Limit Symbol

Indicates the point at which a loop should stop.

## Delay Symbol

Indicates a delay in the process.

### Data Storage or Stored Data Symbol

Indicates a step where data gets stored.

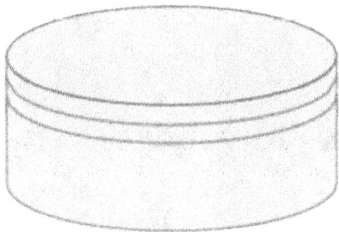

## Database Symbol

Indicates a list of information with a standard structure that allows for searching and sorting.

## Internal Storage Symbol

Indicates that information was stored in memory during a program, used in software design flowcharts.

## Display Symbol

Indicates a step that displays information.

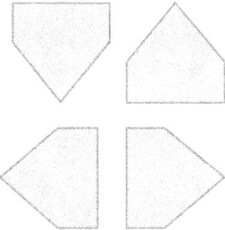

## Off Page

Indicates that the process continues off page.

### ❖  What Is A Flowchart?

A flowchart is a visual representation of the sequence of steps and decisions needed to perform a process. Each step in the sequence is noted within a diagram shape. Steps are linked by connecting lines and directional arrows. This allows anyone to view the flowchart and logically follow the process from beginning to end.

A flowchart is a powerful business tool. With proper design and construction, it communicates the steps in a process very effectively and efficiently.

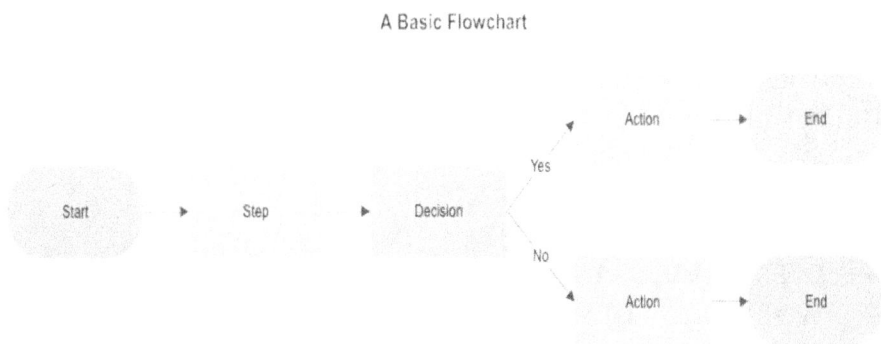

A Basic Flowchart

## ❖ FLOWCHART SYMBOLS

As we know that the flowchart has different shapes and symbols which are used to represent a specific function. which we have studied before, there are two shapes: those with rounded ends represent the start and end points of the process and rectangles are used to show the interim steps. These shapes are known as flowchart symbols.

## How to Make a Flowchart

There are several ways to make a flowchart. Originally, flowcharts were created by hand using pencil and paper. Before the advent of the personal computer, drawing templates made of plastic flowchart shape outlines helped flowchart makers work more quickly and gave their diagrams a more consistent look.

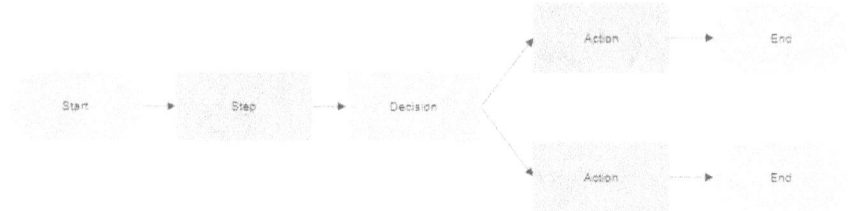

## Types and Uses of Flowcharts

There are a wide variety of **flowchart types**. Here are just a few of the more commonly used ones.

◆ **SWIM LANE FLOWCHARTS**
◆ **DATA FLOW DIAGRAMS**
◆ **INFLUENCE DIAGRAMS**
◆ **WORKFLOW DIAGRAMS**
◆ **PROCESS FLOW DIAGRAMS**
◆ **YES/NO FLOWCHARTS**
◆ **DECISION FLOWS**

*Flowcharts* **were originally used by industrial engineers to structure work processes such as assembly line manufacturing.**
Today, flowcharts are used for a variety of purposes in manufacturing, architecture, engineering, business, technology, education, science, medicine, government, administration and many other disciplines.

*Here are some of the ways flowcharts are used today.*

◆ **PROJECT PLANNING**
◆ **PROGRAM OR SYSTEM DESIGN THROUGH flowchart programming**
◆ **PROCESS DOCUMENTATION**
◆ **AUDIT A PROCESS FOR INEFFICIENCIES OR MALFUNCTIONS**

◆ **MAP COMPUTER ALGORITHMS**
◆ **DOCUMENTING WORKFLOW**

A flowchart is a picture of the separate steps of a process in sequential order. It is a generic tool that can be adapted for a wide variety of purposes, and can be used to describe various processes, such as a manufacturing process, an administrative or service process, or a project plan.

Develop a file to compare two numbers and to report the larger one.

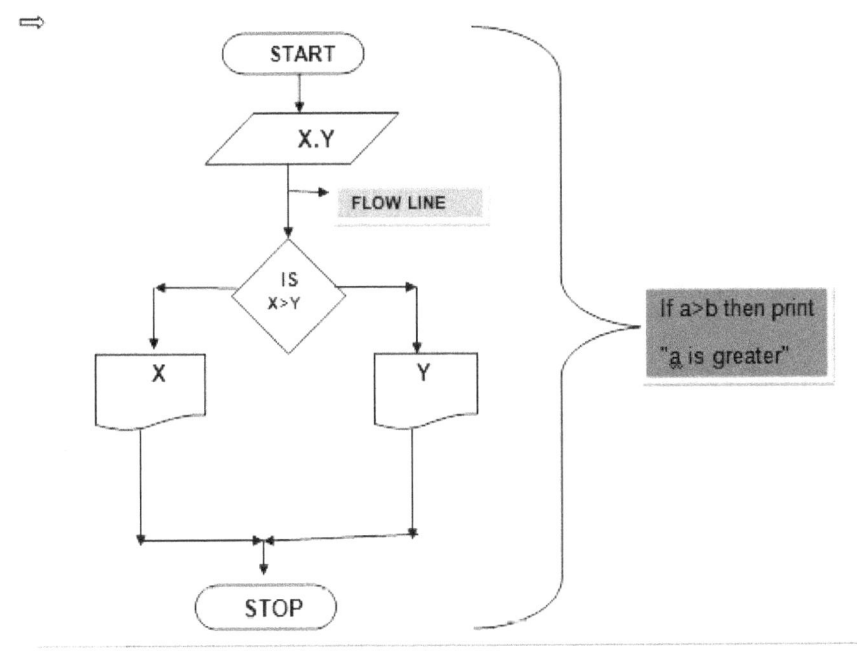

# ELEMENTS OF QBASIC PROGRAMMING

We Must Have To Arrange Some Standard Elements For Constructing The Qbasic Program, The Elements Used In Q-Basic Are As Follows :-

## 1. Keyword

2. Character set

3. Variables

4. Constants

5. Operator and Operands

6. Expression

7. Statements

### 1. KEYWORD

Keywords are those words which have special meanings in QBASIC. Keywords are formed by using characters of QBASIC Characters Set. Keywords are statements, commands, functions (built in functions) and names of operators. The keywords are also called Reserved Words. Some reserved words are CLS, REM, INPUT, LET, PRINT, FOR, DO, SELECT, MID$, ASC, SQR, LEN, LEFT

$, TIME$ and INT.

## 2. Character Set

A set of characters that are allowed to use in QBASIC is known as the QBASIC Character Set. The QBASIC Character Set consists of alphabets (both small and capital), numbers (0 to 9) and special characters. These special characters have their own meaning and function.

*The table below shows the special characters used in QBASIC.*

| Special | Characters | | |
|---|---|---|---|
| ÷ | " | > | $ |
| - | ' | < | % |
| * | . | ( | & |
| / | : | ) | ! |
| \ | : | . | # |
| ^ | – | ? | Blank Space |

QBASIC has the character set consisting
of the following elements:-

Alphabets: A, B, C,....Z , Digits: 0, 1, 2.........,9 and Special characters: + - * / ( ) . , $ ; ,: ,= ,> ,< , ^ .

The symbol ^ (caret) is used to denote exponentiation operator, the symbol * (asterisk) is used to denote multiplication and other symbols; have their usual meanings.

### 3.Variables

The quantity which may change its values during the execution of the program is called the variable.

*In QBASIC, variables are also of two types:*

## 1. *Numeric variable:*

Numeric variable can assume numeric value and is represented by an alphabet or an alphabet followed by another alphabet or digit. For example A, C, A2, ABC, A6 etc, represent numeric variables.

## 2. *String variable:*

A string variable is represented by an alphabet followed by dollar ($)sign. A string variable stores string data. Its type declaration sign is dollar ($).

It should be kept in mind that while constructing the string variable, dollar($)sign should be the last character. For example, B1,NAME, BOOK1$, etc are valid string variables.

## Rules for naming a variable

1. Variable names can have maximum of 40 characters. example {x1,x2,x3,,y1,y2,y3,1,2,3.........}

2. Variable names can have alphabets, numbers and decimal point.

3. A Variable name must begin with a letter.

4. A Variable name cannot begin with fn or FN alphabets. For example, fnames$, fnum etc.

5. Variable names cannot be a reserved words. Example, goto satement

6. Variable names may be ended with type declaration characters like $, %, &, !, and # .
Name$, Address$, Bookname$, GameName$, etc., are examples of Sting Variables.
Salary!, Age%, Mark, Number1, Number2, First Num, Roll Number, etc., are examples of Numeric Variables.

7. variable names are not case sensitive

**Note\*\*\***
*There is no limit on the length of the variable name*
*A variable name cannot contain spaces*
*The variable name cannot be any Go keywords*

## 4. Constants

A quantity in a computer program which does not change its value during the execution of the program is called a constant.

*QBASIC allows the following constants:*

*a) Numeric constant*

- Numeric Constant refers to a number. A number with or without decimal point is a numeric constant. Numeric data should not be enclosed in double quotes. Mathematical operations and logical operations can be performed on the numeric constants. 101, 105.50, 720, 45603, etc. are some examples of numeric constants.
- The numeric constant is one that is formed by a sequence of digits 0, 1, 2,.....9 and may include a decimal point. A numeric constant may be an integer or a real number. 383, +57, 0, -6.2 and 6.15E4 are valid numeric constants.
- The number 6.15E4, in fact, represent 6.15 * 104. The notation E is used to represent the exponential form. The number after E is the exponent which can be positive or negative. However, its length cannot exceed two digits.

- *NOTE \*\* It is also important to keep in mind that:*

*QBASIC does not distinguish between an integer and fraction and Commands are not allowed in a numeric constant.*

***Numeric Constants may be integer, long integer, single precision or double precision.

*Integer* : Integer is whole number between -32768 to 32767.

*Long Integer* : Long Integer is a large range of whole number.

*Single Precision:* Single Precision is seven digit or less than seven digit positive or negative number that contains decimal point. Single Precision can be in the exponential form using E or with a trailing exclamation point. (!). 564, 78.65, 1.2 E-06 and 12345.678! are some examples of Single Precision Constants.

*Double Precision:* Double Precision is 17 digit or less than 17 digit positive or negative numbers that contains decimal point. Double Precision can be in the exponential form using D or with trailing hash sing (#). 9999.99D-12, 2345.786# and 3456.78 are some examples of Double Precision Constants.

The limit on the number of digits that can be used varies from computer to computer. Normally, a numeric constant can have up to a maximum of eight digits.

*b) String constant*
A string constant is an arbitrary sequence of characters that are enclosed in single quotation marks (' '). It is a letter, word, number or a combination of letters with numbers or special character enclosed in double quotes " ". it cannot perform any mathematical operation .For example, 'This is a string'. You can embed single quotation marks in strings by typing two adjacent single quotation marks.

# 5. Operator And Operands

## Operands

Operands are the data or variables on which mathematical, logical and string operations take place.

## Operators

Operators are the symbols, which are used in arithmetic operations, logical expressions, *and* string expressions. these are symbols that indicate the type of operation which are to be performed by QBASIC on the given data or on the values of variables.

There are four types of operators in QBASIC.

1. Arithmetic Operators,
2.Relational Operators
3.Logical Operators
4. String Operators

## a. Arithmetic Operators

Arithmetic Operators are used to perform mathematical calculations like addition, subtraction, division, multiplication and exponential. The following table shows arithmetic operators used in QBASIC.

| Operation | Operator | Example | Result |
|---|---|---|---|
| I . Addition | + | 5+8 | 13 |
| II. Subtraction | - | 8-6 | 2 |
| III. Multiplication | * | 5*4 | 20 |
| IV. Division | / | 8/2 | 4 |
| V. Integer Division | \ | 9\2 | 4 |
| VI. Exponential | ^ | 4^3 | 64 |
| VII. Modular Division | Mod | 7 mod 3 | 1 |

## b. Relational Operators

Relational Operators are use to perform comparisons on two

values of same type. A comparison of sting data with numeric data cannot be done. The comparison of sting data is done on the basis of ASCII value. The result of comparison is either true (non zero) or false (zero). The relational operators are often used to create a test expression that controls program flow. This type of expression is also known as a Boolean expression because they create a Boolean answer or value when evaluated. There are six common relational operators that give a Boolean value by comparing (showing the relationship) between two operands. If the operands are of different data types, implicit promotion occurs to convert the operands to the same data type.

❖ THE FOLLOWING TABLE SHOWS THE RELATIONAL OPERATORS USED IN QBASIC.

| | Operator | Relation | Example |
|---|---|---|---|
| i. | = | Equal to | A = B, A$ = B$ |
| ii. | > | Greater than | A > B, "CAT">"RAT" |
| iii. | < | Less than | A < B, "cat" < "cat" |
| iv. | > = | Greater than or equal to | A > = B, X$ > = Y$ |
| v. | < = | Less than or equal to | A < = B, X$ < = Y$ |
| vi. | < > | Not equal | A$ < > B$, X <> Y. |

# C. Logical Operators -

Logical Operators combine two or more relational expressions to evaluate a single value as True (Non Zero) or False (Zero). The result of evaluation is used to make decisions about the program flow. The commonly used logical operators in QBASIC are AND, OR and NOT.

# 1. And Operator:

AND operator returns 'True' when all the results

returned from individual relational expressions are 'True' otherwise it returns 'False'. The AND Truth Table is given shown below.

| Condition1 (P)---------Condition2 (Q) ---Result (P AND Q) |
|---|
| F ----------------------------- T ----------------------------- F |
| T ----------------------------- F ----------------------------- F |
| F ----------------------------- F ----------------------------- F |
| T ----------------------------- T ----------------------------- T |

*Note\*\*\*: A 'T' indicates a true value and a 'F' indicates a false value.*

# 2. Or Operator:

**OR** *Operator return 'True' if any one of the relational expressions returns 'True'. If all the relational expressions returns 'False' then only the combined result returned by OR operator will be 'False'.*

**The OR Truth table is as given below.**

| Condition 1 (A) ---------------Condition2 (Q) ------------Result (A or B) |
|---|
| F -------------------------------- T -------------------------------- T |
| T -------------------------------- F -------------------------------- T |
| T -------------------------------- T -------------------------------- T |
| F -------------------------------- F -------------------------------- F |

# 3. Not Operator:

**NOT** Operator operates on one operand and returns 'True' if the logical operation returns 'False'.

The **NOT truth table** is as given below.

| Condition1 (A) ---------------Result (NOT A) |
|---|
| F ------------------------------------------------- T |
| T ------------------------------------------------- F |

# D. String Operator -

String Operator joins two or more than two string data. The plus sign (+) is used as the String operator. The act of combining two stings is called concatenation.

The following table shows the use of Sting Operator.

| String Data (A$) | Sting data (B$) | A$ + B$ |
|---|---|---|
| "SIYA" | "RAM" | SIYA RAM |
| "20" | "85" | 2085 |

# 6. Expression

An expression can be a string, or numeric constant, a variable or a combination of constants, variables with operators which returns a single value.

An expression is the combination of operators, constants and variables that is evaluated to get a result. The result of the expression is either string data, numeric data or logical value (true or false) and can be stored in a variable.

For example, the following are expressions in QBASIC.
$(A + B) > C$
$A > = B + C$
$u*t + \frac{1}{2}*a*t^2$

An arithmetic expression may contain more than one operator. While evaluating such expressions, a hierarchy is followed. The hierarchy in arithmetic operations is listed as given below:

*a. Exponentiation (^)*
*b. Negation (-)*
*c. Multiplication and division*
*d. Integer division*
*e. Modular division*
*f. Addition and Subtraction*

The hierarchy in relational operations are =, >, <, <>, < =, and > = respectively. The hierarchy in logical operations are **NOT, AND and OR.**

*NOTE:- When parenthesis is used, it changes the order of hierarchy. The operators inside the parenthesis are evaluated first. So, you can say QBASIC expression follows rule of PEDMAS where P, E, D, M, A and S stand for parenthesis, Exponentiation, Division, Multiplication, Addition, and Subtraction respectively.*

**Algebraic expression cannot be used directly in programming. It must be converted into QBASIC expression.**

Algebraic Expression ----------------------------------- BASIC Expression

A = L × B ------------------------------------------------- A = L * B

P = 2(L + B) ---------------------------------------- P = 2*(L + B)

I = (P × T × R)/100 ------------------------------ I = (P * T * R)/100

V = 4/3 pi R^3 ------------------------------------ V = 4/3 * PI * R^3

# 7. Statements

A statement is a set of instructions written using keywords or commands of QBASIC. Every programming language uses keywords as a statement with certain
syntax. a syntactic unit of an imperative programming language that expresses some action to be carried out.

# Programming

Programming refers to a technological process for telling a computer which tasks to perform in order to solve problems. You can think of programming as a collaboration between humans and computers, in which humans create instructions for a computer to follow (code) in a language computers can understand.

## ❖ ADDITION OF TWO NUMBERS

**10 REM adding two numbers**

**20 INPUT " enter value of first number ", A**

**30 INPUT "enter value of second number", B**

**40 LET C = A + B**

**50 PRINT C**

**60 END**

**Program with its output**

```
19 REM adding two numbers
20 INPUT " enter value of first number ", A
30 INPUT "enter value of second number", B
40 LET C = A + B
50 PRINT C
60 END
```

OUTPUT

```
ter value of first number _
```

```
enter value of first number 4
enter value of second number5_
```

```
enter value of first number 4
enter value of second number5
9
```

Computer programming is the process of performing a particular computation, usually by designing and building an executable computer program. Programming involves tasks such as analysis, generating algorithms, profiling algorithms' accuracy and resource consumption, and the implementation of algorithms.

# STATEMENTS IN Q-BASIC

A statement (for the QBASIC) is **a set of instructions written by using keywords or commands of QBASIC**. Every programming language uses keywords as a statement with certain syntax. The keywords have specific meaning in the QBASIC programming.

A command or set of instructions used in the program is called **statement**. The statement performs specific task in the program. There are several different types statements in QBASIC Programming language. For example, CLS statement clears the screen, PRINT statement displays output and INPUT statement takes the input from the users. In this section we will learn some general statements of QBASIC Programming.

The statements are the first stored in the memory and executed only when the RUN command is given.

## ❖ Different Statements Used In Qbasic Are As Follows:

- **CLS**
- **REM**
- **LET**
- **PRINT**
- **INPUT**

### 1. CLS Statement

The CLS statement clears the screen. If you write CLS statement in the middle of the program then you cannot see the outputs generated before execution of CLS because it clears the screen.

Syntax: CLS

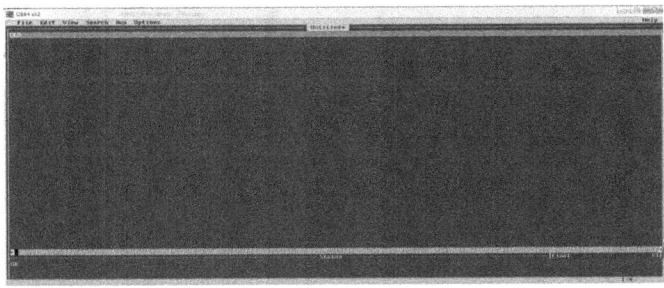

# Rem -

this statement means remark and it can be written anywhere in the program. It is a basic declaration statement that allows explanatory remarks to be inserted in a program. The remarks may be useful in a program to explain about different kinds of statements and user defined words. Adding comments in the program allows us to remind about the program and also helps other programmers to understand the logic of the program.

*Syntax:* **REM < Remarks>**

Syntax : REM

USE OF REM - This statement is used to put comments in the program. It is non-executable statement. We can use (') instead of REM. It increasing readability of program .

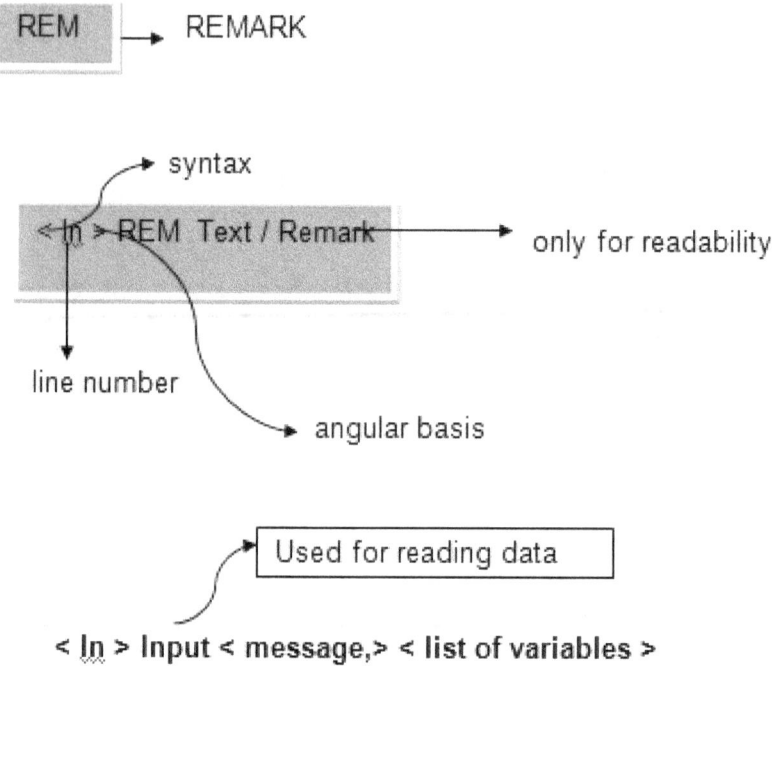

30   INPUT  " enter a number ",  x

## Let -

LET is an assignment statement. It is an an assignment statement which is used to assign value to a variable. LET is an optional statement. It is used to assign the value to a variable. LET is anoptional statement i.e. without using LET statement one can assign the value to a variable. This process is used for data assignment followed by the formula

(READ - DATA - RESTORE)

**The data type must match with the variable type**

## otherwise type mismatch error will occur.

Syntax: |LET| variable = value or expression

## Syntax : Let x = 2

READ - DATA - RESTORE

<LET> - it is used for taking any normalized formula or process .

OPTIONAL

blank space

used for giving blank space

<LET> -  it is used for taking any normalized formula or process .

example:-

INPUT x

< In > blank spce  < LET> blank space

< In > blank space  ( message , list of variables )

Carrier written + line forward

Print " I AM HERE "

Print " YOU ARE THERE "

```
program -
10 REM Test Fire Program
20 Input " Give me a number ", A
30 Input " Enter another number ", B
40  A = A + B
50  B = A - B
60  A = A - B
70 Print " value of A and B = ", A , B
80 END
```

EX. if A = 22 and B = 13  then ,

A + B = 13, 22

Since   A = 22 + 13 = 35

B = 35 - 13 = 13

A = 22 , B = 13

*output*

```
Give me a number 22
Enter another number 13
value of A and B =           13            22
```

*PRINT* - PRINT statement provides output on the screen. It prints the values of the expression on the screen. If the expression list is blank, no characters are printed. The expressions in the list may be numeric or string. In case of number, the negative number is preceded by a minus sign (-) but in positive number it is preceded by a space.

We can use semicolon and comma with a print statement which results differently than a normal PRINT statement. If expression list ends with comma or semicolon, the next PRINT statement prints on the same line. Comma provides a TAB space, but semicolon provides only one space.

Syntax: PRINT ["Message"]; expression.

Example -

CLS
PRINT "all is well."
PRINT
PRINT "life is good."
PRINT 50
PRINT " The number is: "; 40
END

```
CLS
PRINT "all is well."
PRINT
PRINT "life is good."
PRINT 50
PRINT " The number is: "; 40
END
```

*OUTPUT*

all is well
life is good
50
The number is: 40

```
all is well.

life is good.
 50
The number is:  40
```

## INPUT -

> Input reads the value from console and the given value is stored in the variable.

The INPUT statement (the second executable statement of the program on the previous page) provides one way of giving variables (see below for definition) a value. In the example, the INPUT statement is written with a string within lull quotes ("), so that the user is prompted by the computer on what is expected by the program. Input is provided from the standard input device which in this case is the terminal keyboard.

The values for the variables A, B and C can be entered in any convenient free format - with commas or spaces between the numbers, followed by pressing . QuickBasic provides for a far greater flexibility in data input and output which indeed is one of the strengths of the language, but these will not be discussed at this point as they might confuse the newcomer to the language.

Once variables have values, they can be used in assignment statements and/or expressions in the rest of the program to perform desired calculations. A variable must have a value before it is used in an expression or in the right hand side of an assignment statement. example :-

## write a program (wap) for comparing two numbers and to report the greater one.

10 REM COMPARE TWO NUMBERS

20 INPUT "ENTER TWO INTEGERS, "A , B

30 IF A>B THEN PRINT "A" IS GREATER ELSE PRINT "B IS GREATER .

40 PRINT " END OF PROGRAM ***"

This statement is known as terminating or ending program or we can also use stopping program and starting it again.

50 END

# CONTROL STATEMENTS IN QBASIC

Normally programs are executed from top to bottom, in the order that they are written. But sometime it is required to alter the flow of sequence of instructions in a the program. For that QBASIC provide some statements that can alter the flow of a sequence of instructions. The statement which alter and transfer the flow of program from one statement line to another are called control statements.

Mainly, there are two types of control statements in QBASIC. They are:

1. Branching Statement
2. Looping Statement

| Branching Statement | Looping Statement |
|---|---|
| IF ... THEN | FOR .. NEXT |
| IF .. THEN ... ELSE | WHILE ... WEND |
| IF ... THEN ... ELSE IF | DO ... LOOP |
| SELECT ... CASE | NESTED LOOP |
| GOTO | |

Branching Statement also further divided into two types :

- Conditional Branching Statement
  - **IF ... THEN**

- ◦ **IF ... THEN ... ELSE**
- ◦ **IF ... THEN ... ELSE IF**
- ◦ **SELECT CASE**

- • Unconditional Branching Statement

  - ◦ **GOTO**

## 1. IF- statement -

**this statement is used for decision making .**

# 2. if - then < else>

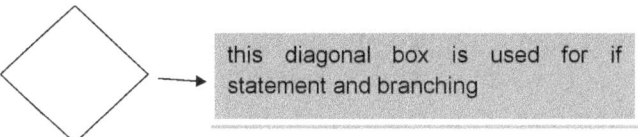

this diagonal box is used for if statement and branching

# 3. IF...THEN...ELSEIF...ELSE

IF (relational condition) THEN STATEMENT(S)
<ELSE STATEMENT(S) -
The IF.....THEN...ELSE IF... ELSE control statement allows identifying if a certain condition is true, and executes a block of code if it is the case. The ELSE clause, while following the "IF 5<9" statement, is associated with the "IF X < 5 " statement, because the "IF 5 < 9 " statement has a PRINT statement on the same line.

## RELATIONAL CONDITIONS

1. > (GREATER THAN)

2. < (LESS THAN)

3. = (EQUALS TO )

4. >= (GREATER THAN EQUAL TO)

5. <=(LESS THAN EQUAL TO )

6. <> ( NOT EQAUL )

**The IF ... THEN ... ELSEIF ... ELSE control statement allows identifying if a certain condition is true, and executes a block of code if it is the case.**

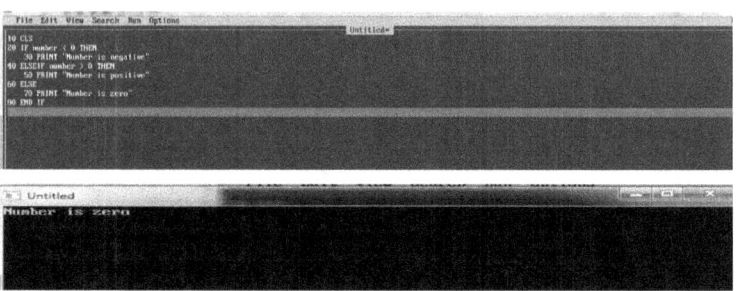

In some implementations of BASIC ( permitted by most versions), the IF statement may need to be contained in one line. However, ELSEIF may not be available in this case, and there is no need for an explicit END IF:

**10 CLS**

**20 IF number<0 THEN PRINT "Number is negative" ELSE PRINT "Number is non-negative"**

This carries over into some implementations of BASIC where if the "IF...THEN" statement is followed by code on the same line then it is fully contained. That is, the compiler assumes the lines ends with "ENDIF", even if it not stated. This is important when dealing with nested "IF...THEN" clauses:

**10 CLS**

**20 IF X<2 THEN**

**30  IF 2<3 THEN PRINT "This is printed if X is 1"**

**40 ELSE**

**50  IF 3<4 THEN PRINT "This is printed if X is 3"**

**60 END IF**

The **ELSE** clause, while following the "IF 2<3" statement, is associated with the "IF X<2" statement, because the "IF 2<3" statement has a PRINT statement on the same line.

For examples

## "if-then-else" programs:-

*1. Input the age of a person and check whether he/she is can vote or not ?*

**Solution -**

- ➢ 10 CLS
- ➢ 20 INPUT AGE 30
- ➢ IF AGE>=18
- ➢ THEN
- ➢ 40 PRINT " CAN VOTE"
- ➢ 50 ELSE
- ➢ 60 PRINT "CAN NOT VOTE"
- ➢ 70 END IF
- ➢ 80 END

*2. Input the age of a person to check if he/she is a senior citizen or not a senior citizen?*

**Solution :-**

- ➢ 10 CLS
- ➢ 20 INPUT AGE
- ➢ 30 IF AGE>=60 THEN
- ➢ 40 PRINT "SENIOR CITIZEN"
- ➢ 50 ELSE
- ➢ 60 PRINT "NOT A SENIOR CITIZEN"
- ➢ 70 END IF
- ➢ 80 END

## WHILE...WEND -

If the condition is true, the code following the WHILE is executed. When the WEND command is executed, it returns control to the WHILE statement (where the condition is tested again). When the condition evaluates to FALSE, control is passed to the statement following the **WEND.**

◆   **SYNTAX**

**The syntax of a While..Wend loop**

**WHILE <condition is true>**

 [do this]

   ..

 [and this]

**WEND**

◆ **FLOW CHART**

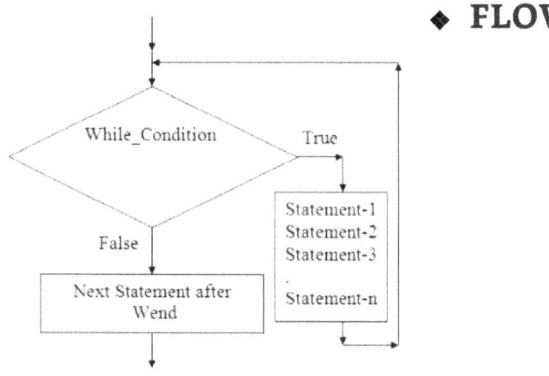

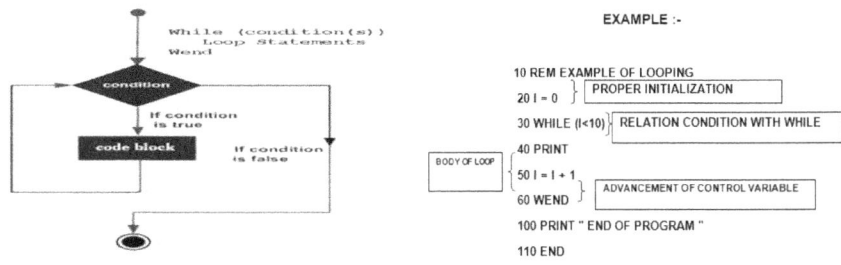

## GOTO -

It is a jumping statement which transfers the control of execution from one line to another . It is a only one unconditional branching statement in QBASIC Programming Language. It transfer the flow of program from one statement line to another statement line without checking any condition.

**Syntax :**

<ln> GOTO line number

Example -

## 60 Goto 20

## ❖ Taking a simple program as an example to understand it better .

10 REM example of looping

20 I = 0

30 IF I > 10 THEN GOTO 100

40 PRINT I

50 I = I + 1

60 GOTO 30

100 PRINT " end of program"

110 END

❖ **ANOTHER SUCH EXAMPLE**

```
CLS
PRINT "welcome"
PRINT "what is your problem"
10 INPUT "write your problem and I'll give you the
solution ", problem$
RANDOMIZE TIMER
PRINT
solution = INT(RND * 4 + 1)
SELECT CASE solution
CASE 1
PRINT "please rephrase your problem."
CASE 2
PRINT "your problem is meaningless."
CASE 3
PRINT "do you think i can give a solution for it?"
CASE 4
PRINT "this problem is not so big."
END SELECT
PRINT
PRINT "enter another problem", K$
GOTO 10
```

*****If a parameter would be covered by more than one case statement, the first option will take priority.******

## Looping -

To make interesting and efficient programs, you can make QBasic to execute a part of a program more than once. This is called looping, when QBasic goes through a part of a program over and over again. This can be done with the GOTO command, but in QBasic there are some good ways to loop the program. One of them is FOR...NEXT command.

**For...next (fixed loop)**

**SYNTAX :-**

**10 FOR I = 10 TO 1  STEP 1**

**20 PRINT I, " HELLO WORLD !"**

**30 NEXT I**

**40 END**

**This command allows you to execute a part of a program for certain number of times. It looks like this:**

This will give an output like this ...

```
I AM STRONG!
I AM STRONG!
I AM STRONG!
I AM STRONG!
I AM STRONG!
```

The letter i can be any other letter, c for example. It is actually a variable, which changes its value each time the program loops (in this example - from 1 to 4). So, if you make a program like this:

```
FOR a = 1 TO 10
    PRINT "This is loop number"; a
NEXT a
```

**THE OUTPUT COMES LIKE THIS**

```
This is loop number 1
This is loop number 2
This is loop number 3
This is loop number 4
This is loop number 5
This is loop number 6
This is loop number 7
This is loop number 8
This is loop number 9
This is loop number 10
```

With **FOR...NEXT** you can use the STEP command, which tells QBasic how to count from one number to another. If you type:

it will count by two : 0, 2, 4, 6, 8, 10, 12

For j = 0 to 6 step 1.5

next j

This will count:
0, 1.5, 3, 4.5, 6

you can also count it backward for instance

For d = 10 to 1 step 1

next d

put step 1 always in q-basic for counting it backward.

## Do...Loop

The **Do - Loop** is basically a repetition of a set of statements to an indefinite number of times, until a condition is satisfied .

for example if you are running a program which works like an ordinary calculator, so if you enter any number. QBasic calculates it and show it's desired result and the program ends. The program may be good, but one problem is that you have to run the program each time if you want to calculate it ! That's where the handy **DO...LOOP** comes in. It's a block of commands, where the program doesn't have to loop a certain number of times, like in **FOR...NEXT**. It can loop indefinitely, while the condition is met (and when it's not met, the loop stops), or until the condition is met (so, when it's met, the loop stops). Condition is basically the same as an argument, for example f < 20. **example:**

**DO**

**PRINT "Enter a number."**

**PRINT "When you want to quit, press 0."**

**INPUT n**

**r = n / 2**

**PRINT n; "/2 ="; r**

**LOOP WHILE n > 0**

**END**

When you run this program, you can enter numbers and get the result as many times as you like. The program loops while numbers you enter are more than 0. Once you've entered 0, the program ends. The condition WHILE n > 0 is put by the LOOP command but you can stick it to the DO command, like that

**DO WHILE n > 0**

**LOOP**

Or you can use the word UNTIL instead, and put it either by DO or LOOP, like that:

**DO UNTIL n = 0**

**LOOP**

**All these examples have the same effect: the program loops while numbers you enter are more than 0 . Then Q-Basic stops looping and goes to execute the command you put after the DO...LOOP block (if it's END command, the program just ends).**

△△△

# PROGRAMING IN QBASIC

**QBASIC** is a programming language which allows
the user to give the desired command in the program
for taking out an output as desired by the user. With a
programming language the complexity of the huge codes
has been simplified in a step by step process. you can tell
the computer what you want it to do. It's a lot like giving
someone directions to your house. The computer follows
each step and does exactly what you desire to do.
with the help of the programs one can easily solve algorithms,
calculations like arithmetic, logical, conditional etc.

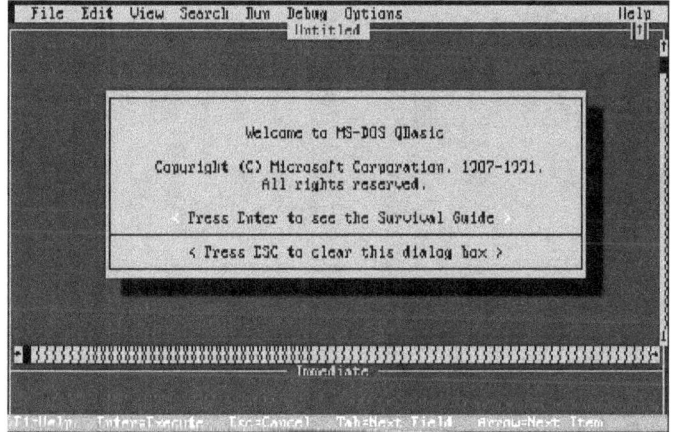

## 1. Write A Program (Wap) To Generate The Following Output Using While-Wend.

solution :-

10 REM TO TEST THE PROGRAM

77

20 I = 10

30 WHILE (I < = 10 )

40 PRINT I , "HELLO"

50 I = I - 1

60 WEND

70 PRINT " END OF JOB "

80 END

# 2 . Write A Program (Wap) To Get 5 Integers From Keyboard And Also Display Them On Screen.

solution : -

10 REM DEMO PROGRAM

20 FOR I = 1 TO 5

30 INPUT " GIVE ME AN INTEGER " , N

40 PRINT " YOU HAVE ENTERED " ; N

50 NEXT I

60 END

# 3 . Write A Program (Wap) To Display The Smallest Number Out Of 10 Integer

# Solution : -

10 REM TO DISPLAY THE SMALLEST NUMBER

20 T = 1000

30 FOR I = 1 TO 10

40 IF T > X THEN T = X

50 NEXT I

60 PRINT " SMALLEST NUMBER IS - " , T

70 END

## 4. Write A Program (Wap) To Display First 50 Even Numbers ( 0,2,4,6,8,....)

## Solution :-

10 REM TO DISPLAY EVEN NUMBERS

20 FOR I = 1 TO 50 STEP 2

30 P = I * 2

40 PRINT P

50 NEXT I

60 END

## 5 . Write A Program (Wap) To Display First 50 Even Numbers And Their Summation

solution : -

10 REM TO DISPLAY SUMMATION

20 S = 0

30 FOR I = 1 TO 50

40 P = 1 * 2

50 PRINT P

60 S = S+ P

70 NEXT I

80 PRINT " SUM = " S

90 END

## 6. Write A Program (Wap) To Read Data .

solution : -

10 REM DEMO OF READ DATA

20 DATA 10,20,30,"MY NAME "

30 DATA 50,100," 1000"

40 READ A,B

50 READ C,D$,E

60 READ F,G&

70 PRINT A,C,B,G$

80 PRINT D$,F,E

90 END

## 7. Write A Program (Wap) To Read 20 Data Items From A Set Of Values . Now You Are Requested To Display Deviation Of Each Data Items From Average Value.

solution : -

10 REM DATA 10,30,50,....95

20 C = 0 ; T = 0

30 FOR I = 1 TO 20

40 READ T

50 C = C + T

60 NEXT I

70 S = C / 20

```
80 FOR I = 1 TO 20
90 READ T
100 PRINT S - T
110 NEXT I
120 END
```

## 8. Write A Program (Wap) To Display Factorial N.

solution : -

```
10 REM TO DISPLAY FACTORIAL N
20 INPUT " ENTER ANY INTEGER " N
30 FACT = 1
40 F OR I = 1 TO N
50 FACT = FACT * I
60 NEXT I
70 PRINT " FACTORIAL = " , FACT
80 END
```

## 9. Write A Program (Wap) To Display 1St To 50 Even Numbers And Their Summation.

solution : -

```
10 REM DEMO PROGRAM
20 T = 0
30 FOR I = 0 TO 49
40 P = I * 2
```

50 PRINT P

60 T = P + T

70 NEXT I

80 PRINT " SUM = " T

90 END

## 10. Write A Program (Wap) To Display Integers From1 To N.

solution : -

10 REM TO DISPLAY INTEGERS FROM 1 TO n

20 INPUT " ENTER THE VALUE OF INTEGER ; N

30 FOR I = 1 TO N

40 PRINT I

50 NEXT I

60 END

△△△

# SORTING IN Q-BASIC

sorting is a method to arrange N elements of arrays in a particular format either ascending or descending in order .

example :-

   int a[10] = {0,11,25,35,14,45,56,77,88,19}

ascending - {0,11,14,19,25,35,45,56,77,88}

descending - {88,77,56,45,35,25,19,14,11,0}


*1. write a program to print **asterisk** " * "*

**program -**

**For K = 1 to 10**

**For I = 1 to 5**

**Print " * ";**

**Next I**

**Print T**

**Next K**

**END**


*program with its output*

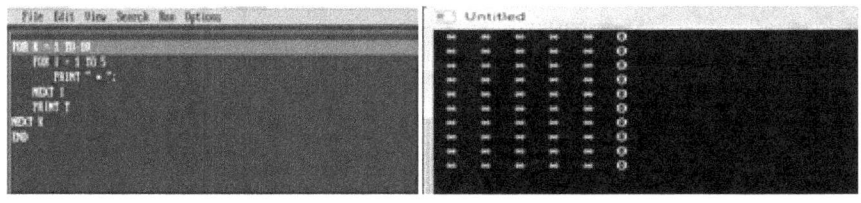

## 2. write a program to print the following pattern

output

11

122

1233

12344

123455

1234566

12345677

123456788

1234567899

1234567891010

program -

For K = 1 to 10

For I = 1 to K

Print I ;

Next I

Print K

Next K

END


*program with its output*

# 3. write a program for the given *pattern*

output

1

22

333

4444

55555

666666

7777777

88888888

999999999

10101010101010101010

program -

**For K = 1 to 10**

**For I = 1 to K**

**Print K ;**

**Next I**

**Print**

**Next K**

**END**

*Program with its output*

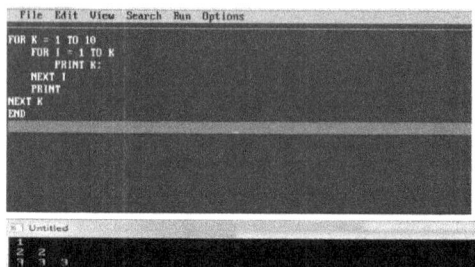

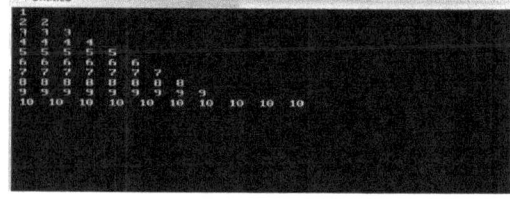

# 4. write a program for the given *pattern*

<u>output</u>

**********

*********

********

*******

******

*****

****

***

**

*

## Program

```
FOR i = 10 TO 1 STEP -1
 FOR j = 1 TO i
 PRINT " * ";
 NEXT j
 PRINT
NEXT i
END
```

*Program with its output*

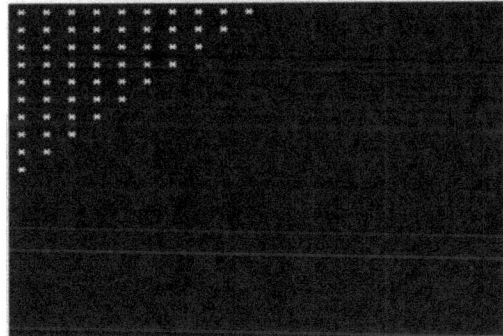

# 5. write a program to print line multiplication table of a number (given by the user )

## program

```
INPUT " Number ? " ; N
For I = 1 to 10
Print I * N
Next I
```

## End

*Program with its output*

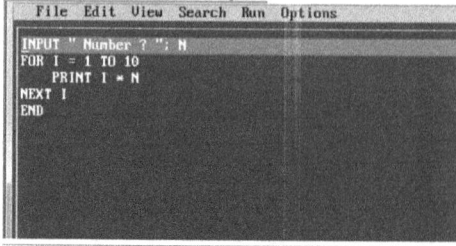

# ******Types Of Shorting********

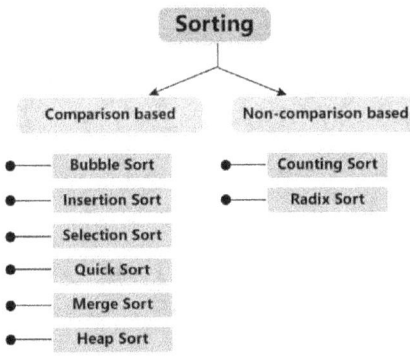

1. bubble sort

2. selection sort

3. insertion sort

4. quick sort

5. merge sort

6. heap sort

7. radix sort

8. self sort

9. tree sort

10. bucket sort

# 1. Bubble Sort

One of the easiest sorts to write is the bubble sort. All this does is use two loops to compare every element of an array with every other element. If one element is bigger than the other it swaps them. for comparing short arrays it's good enough, but because of the number of comparisons it has to do, it's not really suitable for large arrays.

**program for bubble sorting**

```
CLS
REM*PRINT THE ENTERED ELEMENTS IN DECENDING OR ASCENDING ORDER*
PRINT "enter nos of elements"
INPUT n
DIM a(n)
PRINT "enter"; n; "elements"
FOR i = 1 TO n
INPUT a(i)
NEXT i
FOR i = 1 TO n - 1
FOR j = 1 TO n - i
IF a(j) > a(j + 1) THEN
SWAP a(j), a(j + 1)
END IF
NEXT j
NEXT i
FOR i = 1 TO n
PRINT a(i)
NEXT i
END
```

## Program with its output

```
Untitled
enter nos of elements
? 10
enter 10 elements
? 1
? 2
? 3
? 4
? 5
? 6
? 7
? 8
? 9
? 10
  1
  2
  3
  4
  5
  6
  7
  8
  9
  10
Press any key to continue
```

# Write A Program To Sort Numbers In Ascending Order In Qbasic.

*For example,*

Input

1 5 4 3 7 8 9
Output

1 3 4 5 7 8 9

## Steps-

```
CLS
' enter number of numbers you wish to input
INPUT "Enter size of list of numbers: ", n
DIM lst(1 TO n)
PRINT "Enter "; n; " numbers"
FOR i = 1 TO n
  INPUT lst(i)
NEXT i

' displaying input list
PRINT "INPUT NUMBERS:"
FOR i = 1 TO n
  PRINT lst(i);
NEXT i

' sorting lst in ascending order
' using bubble sort
FOR i = 1 TO n
  FOR j = i + 1 TO n
    IF lst(i) > lst(j) THEN
      SWAP lst(i), lst(j)
    END IF
  NEXT j
NEXT i

' displaying output list
```

```
PRINT ""
PRINT "INPUT NUMBERS IN SORTED ORDER:"
FOR i = 1 TO n
  PRINT lst(i);
NEXT i

END
```

# 2. Selection Sort

The repeated selection of the smallest (or largest) element from the unsorted portion of the list and moving it to the sorted portion of the list is termed as **Selection Sort.**
The algorithm repeatedly selects the smallest (or largest) element from the unsorted portion of the list and swaps it with the first element of the unsorted portion.

This process is repeated for the remaining unsorted portion of the list until the entire list is sorted. One variation of selection sort is called "Bidirectional selection sort" which goes through the list of elements by alternating between the smallest and largest element, this way the algorithm can be faster in some cases.

*The algorithm maintains two sub arrays in a given array.*

  · **The sub array which already sorted.**
  · **The remaining sub array was unsorted.**

In every iteration of the selection sort, the minimum element (considering ascending order) from the unsorted sub array is picked and moved to the beginning of the unsorted sub array.

After every iteration sorted sub array size increase by one and the unsorted sub array size decrease by one.

After the N (size of the array) iteration, we will get a sorted array.

# Flowchart Of The Selection Sort:

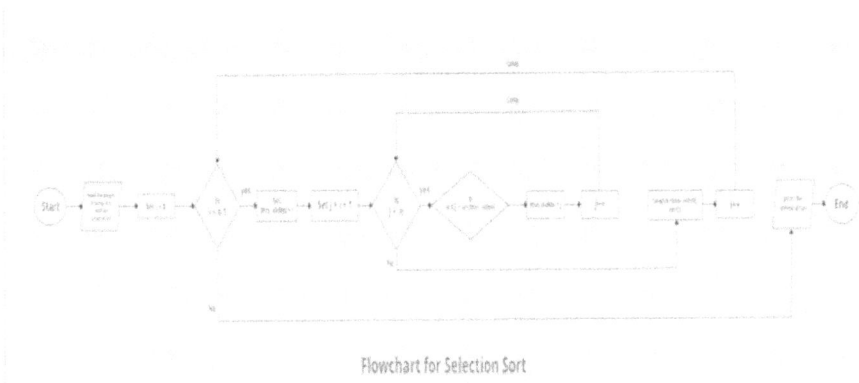

Flowchart for Selection Sort

*Lets us consider the following array as an example:* **arr[] = {54, 25, 12, 22, 10}**

**First pass:**

- *For the first position in the sorted array, the whole array is traversed from index 0 to 4 sequentially. The first position where **54** is stored presently, after traversing whole array it is clear that **10** is the lowest value.*

| 54 | 25 | 12 | 22 | 10 |

- *Thus, replace 64 with 11. After one iteration **10**, which happens to be the least value in the array, tends to appear in the first position of the sorted list.*

| 10 | 25 | 12 | 22 | 54 |

**Second Pass:**

- *For the second position, where 25 is present, again traverse the rest of the array in a sequential manner.*

| 10 | 25 | 12 | 22 | 54 |

- *After traversing, we found that **12** is the second lowest value in the array and it should appear at the second place in the* *array, thus swap these values.*

**10    12    25    22    54**

*Third Pass:*

- *Now, for third place, where* **25** *is present again traverse the rest of the array and find the third least value present in the array.*

**10    12    25    22    54**

- While traversing, **22** came out to be the third least value and it should appear at the third place in the array, thus swap **22** with element present at third position.

**10    12    22    25    54**

**Fourth pass:**

- Similarly, for fourth position traverse the rest of the array and find the fourth least element in the array
- As **25** is the 4th lowest value hence, it will place at the fourth position.

**10    12    22    25    54**

*Fifth Pass:*

- At last the largest value present in the array automatically get placed at the last position in the array
- The resulted array is the sorted array.

**10    12    22    25    54**

Follow the below steps to solve the problem:

- Initialize minimum value(**min_idx**) to location 0.
- Traverse the array to find the minimum element in the array.
- While traversing if any element smaller than **min_idx** is found then swap both values.
- Then, increment **min_idx** to point to the next element.
- Repeat until the array is sorted.

# 3. Insertion Sort

**Insertion sort** is a simple sorting algorithm that works similar to the way you sort playing cards in your hands. The array is virtually split into a sorted and an unsorted part. Values from the unsorted part are picked and placed at the correct position in the sorted part.

**Characteristics of Insertion Sort:**
- This algorithm is one of the simplest algorithm with simple implementation
- Basically, Insertion sort is efficient for small data values
- Insertion sort is adaptive in nature, i.e. it is appropriate for data sets which are already partially sorted.

## Working of Insertion Sort algorithm:
*Consider an example: arr[]: {12, 11, 13, 5, 6}*

| **12** | **11** | **13** | **5** | **6** |

*First Pass:*
- *Initially, the first two elements of the array are compared in insertion sort.*

| **12** | **11** | 13 | 5 | 6 |

- *Here, 12 is greater than 11 hence they are not in the ascending order and 12 is not at its correct position. Thus, swap 11 and 12.*
- *So, for now 11 is stored in a sorted sub-array.*

| **11** | **12** | 13 | 5 | 6 |

*Second Pass:*
**Insertion sort** is a simple sorting algorithm that works similar to the way you sort playing cards in your hands. The array is virtually split into a sorted and an unsorted part. Values from the unsorted part are picked and placed at the correct position

in the sorted part.

**Characteristics of Insertion Sort:**

- This algorithm is one of the simplest algorithm with simple implementation
- Basically, Insertion sort is efficient for small data values
- Insertion sort is adaptive in nature, i.e. it is appropriate for data sets which are already partially sorted.

## Working of Insertion Sort algorithm:

*Consider an example: arr[]: {12, 11, 13, 5, 6}*

| **12** | **11** | **13** | **5** | **6** |

*First Pass:*

- *Initially, the first two elements of the array are compared in insertion sort.*

| **12** | **11** | 13 | 5 | 6 |

- *Here, 12 is greater than 11 hence they are not in the ascending order and 12 is not at its correct position. Thus, swap 11 and 12.*
- *So, for now 11 is stored in a sorted sub-array.*

| **11** | **12** | 13 | 5 | 6 |

*Second Pass:*

- *Now, move to the next two elements and compare them*

| 11 | **12** | **13** | 5 | 6 |

- *Here, 13 is greater than 12, thus both elements seems to be in ascending order, hence, no swapping will occur. 12 also stored in a sorted sub-array along with 11*

*Third Pass:*

- *Now, two elements are present in the sorted sub-array which*

> *are **11** and **12***
- *Moving forward to the next two elements which are 13 and 5*

| 11 | 12 | **13** | **5** | 6 |
|----|----|----|----|----|

- *Both 5 and 13 are not present at their correct place so swap them*

| 11 | 12 | **5** | **13** | 6 |
|----|----|----|----|----|

- *After swapping, elements 12 and 5 are not sorted, thus swap again*

| 11 | **5** | **12** | 13 | 6 |
|----|----|----|----|----|

- *Here, again 11 and 5 are not sorted, hence swap again*

| **5** | **11** | 12 | 13 | 6 |
|----|----|----|----|----|

- *Here, 5 is at its correct position*

## Fourth Pass:

- *Now, the elements which are present in the sorted sub-array are **5**, **11** and **12***
- *Moving to the next two elements 13 and 6*

| 5 | 11 | 12 | **13** | **6** |
|----|----|----|----|----|

- *Clearly, they are not sorted, thus perform swap between both*

| 5 | 11 | 12 | **6** | **13** |
|----|----|----|----|----|

- *Now, 6 is smaller than 12, hence, swap again*

| 5 | 11 | **6** | **12** | 13 |
|----|----|----|----|----|

- *Here, also swapping makes 11 and 6 unsorted hence, swap again*

| 5 | **6** | **11** | 12 | 13 |
|----|----|----|----|----|

• *Finally, the array is completely sorted.*

## *Illustrations:*

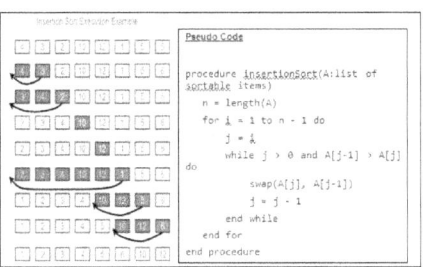

This algorithm sorts an array of items by repeatedly taking an element from the unsorted portion of the array and inserting it into its correct position in the sorted portion of the array.

1. The procedure takes a single argument, '**A**', which is a list of sort-able items.
2. The variable 'n' is assigned the length of the array A.
3. The outer for loop starts at index '**1**' and runs for '**n-1**' iterations, where '**n**' is the length of the array.
4. The inner while loop starts at the current index i of the outer for loop and compares each element to its left neighbor. If an element is smaller than its left neighbor, the elements are swapped.
5. The inner while loop continues to move an element to the left as long as it is smaller than the element to its left.
6. Once the inner while loop is finished, the element at the current index is in its correct position in the sorted portion of the array.
7. The outer for loop continues iterating through the array until all elements are in their correct positions and the array is fully sorted.

<u>**Insertion Sort Algorithm**</u>

To sort an array of size N in ascending order:
- Iterate from arr[1] to arr[N] over the array.
- Compare the current element (key) to its predecessor.
- If the key element is smaller than its predecessor, compare it to the elements before. Move the greater elements one position up to make space for the swapped element.

# 4. Quick Sort

Quick sort is **a fast sorting algorithm that works by splitting a large array of data into smaller sub-arrays**. This implies that each iteration works by splitting the input into two components, sorting them, and then recombining them.

Like **Merge Sort, Quick Sort** is a Divide and Conquer algorithm. It picks an element as a pivot and partitions the given array around the picked pivot. There are many different versions of quick Sort that pick pivot in different ways.

- Always pick the first element as a pivot.
- Always pick the last element as a pivot (implemented below)
- Pick a random element as a pivot.
- Pick median as the pivot.

The key process in **quick Sort** is a partition(). The target of partitions is, given an array and an element x of an array as the pivot, put x at its correct position in a sorted array and put all smaller elements (smaller than x) before x, and put all greater elements (greater than x) after x. All this should be done in linear time.

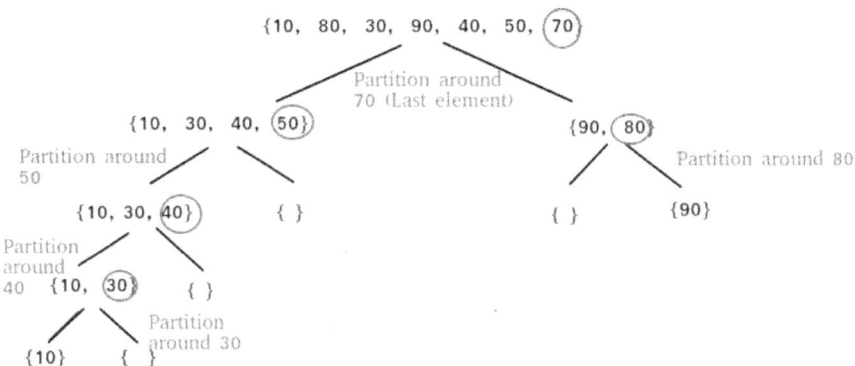

## Pseudo code for partition()

/* This function takes last element as pivot, places the pivot element at its correct position in sorted array, and places all smaller (smaller than pivot) to left of pivot and all greater elements to right of pivot */

partition (arr[], low, high)
{
　// pivot (Element to be placed at right position)
　pivot = arr[high];


　i = (low – 1) // Index of smaller element and indicates the
　// right position of pivot found so far
　for (j = low; j <= high- 1; j++)
　{
　　// If current element is smaller than the pivot
　　if (arr[j] < pivot)

　　{
　　　i++;   // increment index of smaller element

```
      swap arr[i] and arr[j]
   }
 }

      swap arr[i + 1] and arr[high])
  return (i + 1)
}
```

## Illustration of partition() :

Consider: arr[] = {10, 80, 30, 90, 40, 50, 70}

- Indexes: 0  1  2  3  4  5  6
- low = 0, high =  6, pivot = arr[h] = 70
- Initialize index of smaller element, **i = -1**

**Counter variables**
I: Index of smaller element
J: Loop variable

We start the loop with initial values

| Test Condition<br>arr [J] <= pivot | Actions | Value of variables<br>I = -1<br>J = 0 |
|---|---|---|

- Traverse elements from j = low to high-1
    - **j = 0**: Since arr[j] <= pivot, do i++ and swap(arr[i], arr[j])
    - **i = 0**
- arr[] = {10, 80, 30, 90, 40, 50, 70} // No change as i and j are same
- **j = 1**: Since arr[j] > pivot, do nothing

## Partition

**Counter variables**
I: Index of smaller element
J: Loop variable

Pass 2

| Test Condition | Actions | Value of variables |
|---|---|---|
| arr [J] <= pivot | | I = 0 |
| 80 < 70 false | No Action | J = 1 |

- **j = 2** : Since arr[j] <= pivot, do i++ and swap(arr[i], arr[j])
- **i = 1**
- arr[] = {10, 30, 80, 90, 40, 50, 70} // We swap 80 and 30

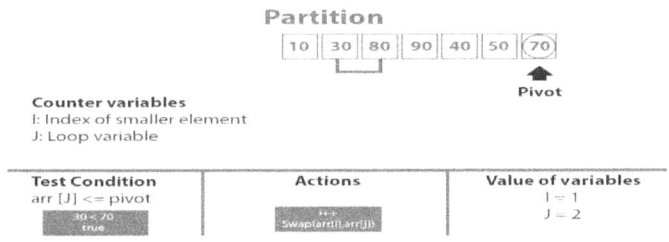

**Counter variables**
I: Index of smaller element
J: Loop variable

| Test Condition | Actions | Value of variables |
|---|---|---|
| arr [J] <= pivot | | I = 1 |
| 30 < 70 true | i++ Swap(arr[i],arr[j]) | J = 2 |

- **j = 3** : Since arr[j] > pivot, do nothing // No change in i and arr[]
- **j = 4** : Since arr[j] <= pivot, do i++ and swap(arr[i], arr[j])
- **i = 2**
- arr[] = {10, 30, 40, 90, 80, 50, 70} // 80 and 40 Swapped

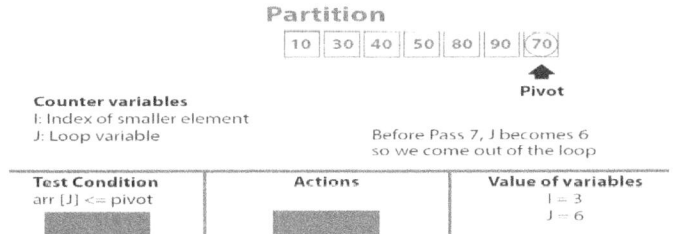

**Counter variables**
I: Index of smaller element
J: Loop variable

Before Pass 7, J becomes 6 so we come out of the loop

| Test Condition | Actions | Value of variables |
|---|---|---|
| arr [J] <= pivot | | I = 3 |
| | | J = 6 |

- We come out of loop because j is now equal to high-1.

- **Finally we place pivot at correct position by swapping arr[i+1] and arr[high] (or pivot)**
- arr[] = {10, 30, 40, 50, 70, 90, 80} // 80 and 70 Swapped

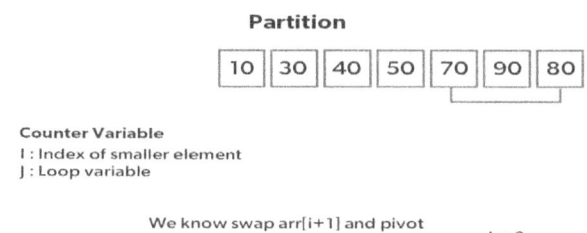

**Partition**

| 10 | 30 | 40 | 50 | 70 | 90 | 80 |

Counter Variable
I : Index of smaller element
J : Loop variable

We know swap arr[i+1] and pivot

I = 3

- Now 70 is at its correct place. All elements smaller than 70 are before it and all elements greater than 70 are after it.
- Since quick sort is a recursive function, we call the partition function again at left and right partitions

**Quick sort left**

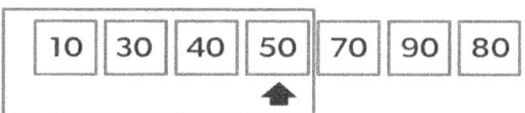

| 10 | 30 | 40 | 50 | 70 | 90 | 80 |

Since quick sort is a recursion function,
wecall the Partition function again

First 50 is the pivot.

As it is already at its correct position
we call the quicksort function again on the left part.

- Again call function at right part and swap 80 and 90

**Quick sort Right**

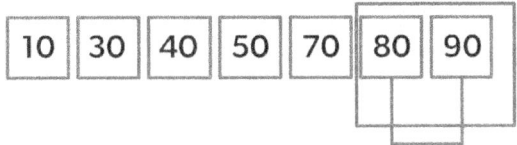

80 is the Pivot

80 and 90 are swapped to bring pivot
to correct position

# 5. Merge Sort

A merge sort **uses a technique called divide and conquer**. The list is repeatedly divided into two until all the elements are separated individually. Pairs of elements are then compared, placed into order and combined. The process is then repeated until the list is recompiled as a whole.

It is one of the most popular and efficient sorting algorithm. It divides the given list into two equal halves, calls itself for the two halves and then merges the two sorted halves. We have to define the **merge()** function to perform the merging. The sub-lists are divided again and again into halves until the list cannot be divided further. Then we combine the pair of one element lists into two-element lists, sorting them in the process. The sorted two-element pairs is merged into thc four-element lists, and so on until we get the sorted list.

Now, let's see the algorithm of merge sort.

## ❖ ALGORITHM

In the following algorithm, **arr** is the given array, **beg** is the starting element, and **end** is the last element of the array.

- ❖ MERGE_SORT(arr, beg, end)

- ❖ if beg < end
- ❖ set mid = (beg + end)/2
- ❖ MERGE_SORT(arr, beg, mid)
- ❖ MERGE_SORT(arr, mid + 1, end)
- ❖ MERGE (arr, beg, mid, end)
- ❖ end of if

## ❖ END MERGE_SORT

The important part of the merge sort is the **MERGE** function. This function performs the merging of two sorted sub-arrays that are **A[beg...mid]** and **A[mid+1...end]**, to build one sorted array **A[beg...end]**. So, the inputs of the **MERGE** function are **A[]**, **beg, mid,** and **end**.

The implementation of the MERGE function is given as follows -

```
1. /* Function to merge the subarrays of a[] */
2. void merge(int a[], int beg, int mid, int end)
3. {
4. int i, j, k;
5. int n1 = mid - beg + 1;
6. int n2 = end - mid;

7. int    LeftArray[n1],    RightArray[n2];    // temporary arrays

8. /* copy data to temp arrays */
9. for (int i = 0; i < n1; i++)
   10. LeftArray[i] = a[beg + i];
   11. for (int j = 0; j < n2; j++)
   12. RightArray[j] = a[mid + 1 + j];

   13. i = 0, /* initial index of first sub-array */
```

14. j = 0; /* initial index of second sub-array */
15. k = beg;   /* initial index of merged sub-array */

16. while (i < n1 && j < n2)
17. {
18. if(LeftArray[i] <= RightArray[j])
19. {

a. a[k] = LeftArray[i];
b. i++;
20. }
21. else
22. {
        a. a[k] = RightArray[j];
        b. j++;
23. }
24. k++;
25. }
26. while (i<n1)
27. {
28. a[k] = LeftArray[i];
29. i++;
30. k++;
31. }
32. while (j<n2)
33. {
34. a[k] = RightArray[j];
35. j++;
36. k++;
37. }
38. }

## ◆ WORKING OF MERGE SORT ALGORITHM

Now, let's see the working of merge sort Algorithm.

To understand the working of the merge sort algorithm, let's take an unsorted array. It will be easier to understand the merge sort via an example.

Let the elements of array are -

| 12 | 31 | 25 | 8 | 32 | 17 | 40 | 42 |

According to the merge sort, first divide the given array into two equal halves. Merge sort keeps dividing the list into equal parts until it cannot be further divided.

As there are eight elements in the given array, so it is divided into two arrays of size 4.

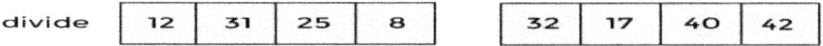

Now, again divide these two arrays into halves. As they are of size 4, so divide them into new arrays of size 2.

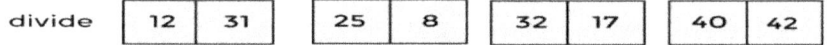

Now, again divide these arrays to get the atomic value that cannot be further divided.

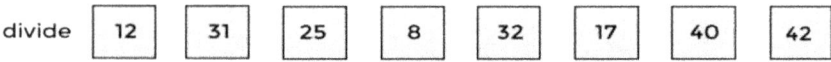

Now, combine them in the same manner they were broken.

In combining, first compare the element of each array and then combine them into another array in sorted order.

So, first compare 12 and 31, both are in sorted positions. Then compare 25 and 8, and in the list of two values, put 8 first followed by 25. Then compare 32 and 17, sort them and put 17 first followed by 32. After that, compare 40 and 42, and place them sequentially.

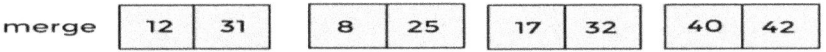

In the next iteration of combining, now compare the arrays with two data values and merge them into an array of found values in sorted order.

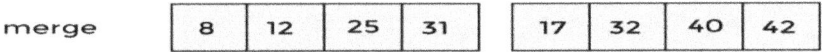

Now, there is a final merging of the arrays. After the final merging of above arrays, the array will look like -

| 8 | 12 | 17 | 25 | 31 | 32 | 40 | 42 |

Now, the array is completely sorted.

## ❖ MERGE SORT COMPLEXITY

Now, let's see the time complexity of merge sort in best case, average case, and in worst case. We will also see the space complexity of the merge sort.

1. Time Complexity

| Case | Time Complexity |
|------|-----------------|
| Best Case | O(n*logn) |
| Average Case | O(n*logn) |
| Worst Case | O(n*logn) |

- **Best Case Complexity** - It occurs when there is no sorting required, i.e. the array is already sorted. The best-case time complexity of merge sort is **O(n*logn)**.

- **Average Case Complexity** - It occurs when the array elements are in jumbled order that is not properly ascending and not properly descending. The average case time complexity of merge sort is **O(n*logn)**.

- **Worst Case Complexity** - It occurs when the array elements are required to be sorted in reverse order. That means suppose you have to sort the array elements in ascending order, but its elements are in descending order. The worst-case time complexity of merge sort is **O(n*logn)**.

2. Space Complexity

| Space Complexity | O(n) |
|---|---|
| Stable | YES |

*****The space complexity of merge sort is O(n). It is because, in merge sort, an extra variable is required for swapping.*****

# 6. Heap Sort

Heap sort can be defined as an improved selection sort: like selection sort, heap sort divides its input into a sorted and an unsorted region, and it iteratively shrinks the unsorted region by extracting the largest element from it and inserting it into the sorted region. in other words it is a comparison-based sorting technique based on Binary Heap data structure. It is similar to the selection sort where we first find the minimum element and place the minimum element at the beginning. Repeat the same process for the remaining elements.

The heap sort algorithm can be divided into two parts.

In the first step, a heap is built out of the data (see Binary heap § Building a heap). The heap is often placed in an array with the layout of a complete binary tree. The complete binary tree maps the binary tree structure into the array indices; each array index represents a node; the index of the node's parent, left child branch, or right child branch are simple expressions. For a zero-based array, the root node is stored at index 0; if i is the index of the current node, then

**iParent(i)   = floor((i-1) / 2) where floor functions map a real number to the largest leading integer.**

    **iLeftChild(i) = 2*i + 1**
    **iRightChild(i) = 2*i + 2**

In the second step, a sorted array is created by repeatedly removing the largest element from the heap (the root of the heap), and inserting it into the array. The heap is updated after each removal to maintain the heap property. Once all objects have been removed from the heap, the result is a sorted array.

Array = {1, 3, 5, 4, 6, 13, 10, 9, 8, 15, 17}

Corresponding Complete Binary Tree is:

```
            1
         /    \
       3       5
      / \    / \
     4   6  13  10
    /\  /\
   9 8 15 17
```

**The task to build a Max-Heap from above array**.

Total Nodes = 11.

Total non-leaf nodes= (11/2)-1=5

last non-leaf node = 6.

Therefore, Last Non-leaf node index = 4.

To build the heap, heapify only the nodes: [1, 3, 5, 4, 6] in reverse order.

**Heapify 6**: Swap 6 and 17.

```
          1
       /   \
      3     5
     / \   / \
    4   17 13 10
   / \  / \
  9 8 15 6
```

**Heapify 4**: Swap 4 and 9.

```
          1
       /   \
      3     5
     / \   / \
    9   17 13 10
   / \  / \
  4 8 15 6
```

**Heapify 5**: Swap 13 and 5.

```
          1
       /   \
      3     13
     / \   / \
    9   17 5 10
   / \  / \
  4 8 15 6
```

**Heapify 3**: First Swap 3 and 17, again swap 3 and 15.

```
         1
      /  \
    17     13
   / \   / \
  9  15 5 10
 /\  / \
4 8 3 6
```

**Heapify 1**: First Swap 1 and 17, again swap 1 and 15, finally swap 1 and 6.

```
       17
      /  \
    15     13
   / \   / \
  9   6 5 10
 /\  / \
4 8 3  1
```

# Advantages Of Heap Sort:

- Efficiency – The time required to perform Heap sort increases logarithmically while other algorithms may grow exponentially slower as the number of items to sort increases. This sorting algorithm is very efficient.

- Memory Usage – Memory usage is minimal because apart from what is necessary to hold the initial list of items to be sorted, it needs no additional memory space to work.

- Simplicity – It is simpler to understand than other equally efficient sorting algorithms because it does not use advanced computer science concepts such as recursion.

# Disadvantages Of Heap Sort:

- Costly: Heap sort is costly.
- Unstable: Heap sort is unstable. It might rearrange the relative order.
- Efficient: Heap Sort are not very efficient when working with highly complex data.

# Applications Of Heap Sort:

- Heap sort is mainly used in hybrid algorithms like the Intro Sort.
- Sort a nearly sorted (or K sorted) array
- k largest(or smallest) elements in an array

# 7. Radix Sort

Radix sort is a non-comparison-based sorting algorithm. The word radix, by definition, refers to the base or the number of unique digits used to represent numbers. In radix sort, we sort the elements by processing them in multiple passes, digit by digit. Each pass sorts elements according to the digits in a particular place value, using a stable sorting algorithm (usually counting sort as a subroutine). It can be implemented to start the sorting from the least significant digit (LSD) or the most significant digit (MSD).

# Applications Of Radix Sort

1. Here are a few applications of the radix sort algorithm:

2. Radix sort can be applied to data that can be sorted lexicographically, such as words and integers. It is also used for stably sorting strings.

3. It is a good option when the algorithm runs on parallel machines, making the sorting faster. To use parallelization, we divide the input into several buckets, enabling us to sort the buckets in parallel, as they are independent of each other.

4. It is used for constructing a suffix array. (An array that contains all the possible suffixes of a string in sorted order is called a suffix array. For example: If the string is "sort," then the suffix array SA[] will be:

| | |
|---|---|
| SA[0] | = "or" |
| SA[1] | = "ort" |
| SA[2] | = "sort" |
| SA[3] | = "t" |

# ◆ Radix Sort Algorithm

the algorithm for radix sort:

Radix Sort (Array, size Array)

**Step 1:** Find the largest element in the unsorted input array (Array)

**Step 2:** Create a for expression that loops d times, where d = number of digits in the largest element (maxim)

**Step 3:** For the first place value, call counting sort, jump place value by 10 to move to the next significant digit

**Step 4:** Continue step 3 for all place values (finish all d passes)

**Step 5:** Print out the updated, sorted array.

**Step 6:** Exit

# Radix Sort Pseudo Code

- Following is the pseudo code for radix sort. Use this to implement radix sort in any programming language of your choice.
- radix Sort()
- Find largest element (maxim) in the input array array[]
- For each place value in input (place=1;maxim/place>0;place*=10)
- Sort all elements on the basis of digits in that place value
- using counting sort
- For each array[] index (i=0;i<size;i++)
- Store all the sorted elements in the original array
- Output the sorted array[]
- end radixSort()

# 8. Self Sort

A self-organizing list is a list that reorders its elements based on some self-organizing heuristic to improve average access time. The aim of a self-organizing list is to improve efficiency of linear search by moving more frequently accessed items towards the head of the list. A self-organizing list achieves near constant time for element access in the best case. A self-organizing list uses a reorganizing algorithm to adapt to various query distributions at runtime.

# Applications Of Self-Organizing Lists

Language translators like compilers and interpreters use self-organizing lists to main-tain symbol tables during compilation or interpretation of program source code. Currently research is underway to incorporate the self-organizing list data structure in embedded systems to reduce bus transition activity which leads to power dissipation in those circuits. These lists are also used in artificial intelligence and neural net-works as well as self-adjusting programs.

The algorithms used in self-organizing lists are also used as caching algorithms as in the case of LFU algorithm.

The simple Move to Front and transpose methods are also applicable in real-world col-lections: for instance organizing a spice drawer by replacing used items to the front of a drawer, or transposing a cleaning item with its front-most neighbor when it is used.

# 9. Tree Sort

Tree sort is a sorting algorithm that is based on Binary Search Tree data structure. It first creates a binary search tree from the elements of the input list or array and then performs an in-order traversal on the created binary search tree to get the elements in sorted order.

# Algorithm:

step 1.  Take the elements input in an array.

step 2.  Create a Binary search tree by inserting data items from thc array into the binary search tree.

step 3.  Perform in-order traversal on the tree to get the elements in sorted order.

## Applications of Tree sort:

1. Its most common use is to edit the elements online: after each installation, a set of objects seen so far is

available in a structured program.

2. If you use a splay tree as a binary search tree, the resulting algorithm (called splay sort) has an additional property that it is an adaptive sort, which means its working time is faster than O (n log n) for virtual inputs.

# 10. Bucket Sort

Bucket sort is mainly useful when input is uniformly distributed over a range.
For example, consider the following problem.
Sort a large set of floating point numbers which are in range from 0.0 to 1.0 and are uniformly distributed across the range.

## working -

A simple way is to apply a comparison based sorting algorithm. The lower bound for Comparison based sorting algorithm (Merge Sort, Heap Sort, Quick-Sort etc) is $\Omega(n \log n)$, i.e., they cannot do better than nLogn .
Can we sort the array in linear time? Counting sort can not be applied here as we use keys as index in counting sort. Here keys are floating point numbers. The idea is to use bucket sort.

## Bucket Sort Algorithm.

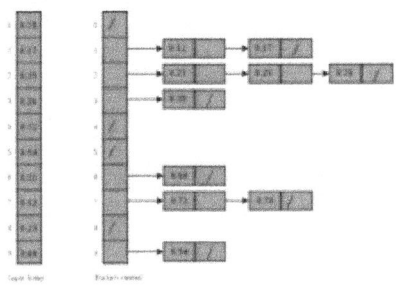

bucketSort(arr[], n)
1) Create n empty buckets (Or lists).
2) Do following for every array element arr[i].
.......a) Insert arr[i] into bucket[n*array[i]]
3) Sort individual buckets using insertion sort.
4) Concatenate all sorted buckets.

**Q-basic is an IDE(integrated development environment) developed by Microsoft to create, edit, debug and execute basic program.**

# Built-In Types

Q- Basic has five built-in types of arrays they are:- INTEGER (%), LONG(&) integer, SINGLE(!) float, DOUBLE(#) float and STRING($). QB64 has two more built-in types: _INTEGER64 (&&) and _FLOAT (##)

Implicit declaration is by adding the type character to the end of the variable name (%, &, !, #, $, &&, ##). See **QBasic/Basic math** for more.

Explicit declaration is by using the **DIM** statement before first use:

    DIM a AS STRING
    DIM b AS INTEGER
    DIM c AS LONG
    DIM d AS SINGLE
    DIM e AS DOUBLE
    DIM f AS _INTEGER64 'QB64 only
    DIM g AS _FLOAT 'QB64 only

If you do not use either implicit or explicit declaration, QBASIC interpreter assumes SINGLE type.

1 Built-in Types
2 User-defined type
3 Array
4 Multidimensional array
5 Non-zero base

## User-Defined Type

A user defined type allows you to create your own data structures. Please note that custom types are similar to arrays.

```
TYPE studenttype
  name AS STRING
  score AS INTEGER
END TYPE
```

You can then declare variables under this type, and access them:

```
DIM studentname AS studenttype
studentname.name = "Bob"
studentname.score = 92
```

This above example shows how a custom type can be used for maintaining data of a

student .

ΔΔΔ

# ARRAYS IN Q-BASIC

An array is a subscripted numeric variable or a group of similar types of variables which have a symbol followed by the index or subscript . This subscript has some integer numeric value . Array is a collection of values stored in a single variable.

**SYNTAX :-**

**DIM ARRAY NAME (SIZE) AS DATA TYPE**

**DIM F NAMES (5) AS STRING**

**NOTE\*\* To declare an array DIM (dimension) statement is used.**

Here "DIM" is a keyword to declare array, similarly 'numbers' is a name of array. If you want to create a string array variable then you need to add dollar ($) at the end of the name of array variable. 10 inside the parentheses means this array can hold 11 elements, yes 11 elements there is a first index array 0 also (0 to 10), but it can store only number value because 'numbers' is a numerical variable.

A string is also an array of characters (for example, char$(1) means 1st character in string char$). Arrays of numbers should be defined using the dim instruction (unless you dim them, they are limited to 10 elements on each dimension).

By default, arrays in q- basic are static in size and cannot be changed later in the program.

code that will set up this type of array is as follows:

**DIM myArray(10) as TYPE 'this is explaining the data type to be used during program execution in array'**

**Type** can be any of the predefined in q-basic (integer, long, single, double, string) or user-defined type. If this is not specified, the array takes the type defined by the variable name suffix - integer (%), long(&) integer, single(!) Float, double(#), string($) - or integer if none.

note*** :- if your data type is string, dim string(10) defines a single string of 10 characters, not 10 strings of arbitrary length ! (10 strings of up to 128 chars each would be defined as dim string(10,128)

By issuing the meta command '$dynamic at the beginning of your program you can cause your arrays to be dynamic: '
**$DYNAMIC**

**DIM myDynamicArray(5) as INTEGER**
**REDIM myDynamicArray(10) as INTEGER**

This is now perfectly legal code.

To free up space occupied by an array, use the **ERASE statement**. taking an example

**For I = 1 to 10**

**Input X(I)**

**Next I**

**For I = 1 to 10**

Print X(I)

Next I

END

# Multidimensional Array

An array isn't restricted to one dimension - it's possible to declare an array to accept two parameters in order to represent a grid of values.

```
DIM house names(25,25) as STRING
```

You cannot use the REDIM statement to change the number of dimensions on the array, even with dynamic allocation.

### Non-zero base

In most languages, arrays start at the value 0, and count up. In basic, it's possible to index arrays so that they start at any value, and finish at any other value.

```
DIM deltas(-5 TO 5)
```

you can change the default lower bound with the option base statement.

# ❖ Some More Examples Based On This Are As Following

# 1. Write A Program (Wap) To Input 10 Names Display Them On The Screen.

```
Dim N$(10)
Print " Enter 10 Names "
For I = 1 to 10
Input X$(I)
Next I
For I = 1 TO 10
Print X$(I)
Next I
End
```

## 2. Write A Program (Wap) To Find Greatest Among 5 Numbers Using Array

```
CLS

DIM num(4)

PRINT "Enter any any 5 numbers"

FOR j = 0 TO 4

INPUT num(j)

NEXT j

lrg = num(0)

FOR j = 0 TO 4

IF lrg > num(j) THEN

lrg = num(j)

END IF

NEXT j

PRINT "largest number is="; lrg

END
```

# 3. Write A Program To Input Name And Marks And Display It On Screen Using Array

```
CLS
DIM n$(5)
DIM m(5)
PRINT "Enter Name and Marks of any 5 students"
FOR i = 1 TO 5
PRINT i
INPUT "Enter Name: "; n$(i)
INPUT "Enter Marks:"; m(i)
NEXT i
PRINT
PRINT
PRINT
PRINT "MARKS OF STUDENTS"
PRINT "NAME", "MARKS", "RESULT"
FOR i = 1 TO 5
IF m(i) >= 40 THEN
r$ = "PASSED"
ELSE
r$ = "FAILED"
END IF
PRINT n$(i), m(i), r$
NEXT i
END
```

# 4. Write A Program To Display Name And Roll Number Using Read Data

```
DIM n$(6), rn(6)
CLS
FOR i = 0 TO 6
READ n$(i), rn(i)
```

```
NEXT i
FOR i = 0 TO 6
PRINT n$(i), rn(i)
NEXT i
DATA
RAM,2,SHYAM,5,ADITYA,3,SURESH,8,KESHAV,9,RAMYA,10,SUDHEER,11
END
```

# 5. Write A Program To Sort Name In Ascending Order

```
CLS
REM*SORTING OF STRING*
PRINT "ENTER NO OF ELEMENTS"
INPUT N
DIM A$(N)
PRINT "ENTER "; N; "NAMES"
FOR I = 1 TO N
INPUT A$(I)
NEXT I
FOR I = 1 TO N – 1
FOR J = 1 TO N – I
IF A$(J) > A$(J + 1) THEN
SWAP A$(J), A$(J + 1)
END IF
NEXT J
NEXT I
PRINT "AFTER SORTING"
FOR I = 1 TO N
```

```
PRINT A$(I)
NEXT I
END
```

# 6. Write A Program To Do The Matrix Addition

```
Cls
Rem*Addition Of Matrix*
Input "Enter Row"; R
Input "Enter Column"; C
Dim M1(R, C), M2(R, C)
Print "Enter Matrix M1"
For I = 1 To R
For J = 1 To C
Input M1(I, J)
Next J
Next I
Print "Enter Matrix M2"
For I = 1 To R
For J = 1 To C
Input M2(I, J)
Next J
```

```
Next I
For I = 1 To R
For J = 1 To C
M3(I, J) = M1(I, J) + M2(I, J)
Next J
Next I
Print "Addtion Of Matrix"
For I = 1 To C
For J = 1 To R
Print M3(I, J);
Next J
Print
Next I
End
```

△△△

# CONCEPT OF MODULAR PROGRAMMING

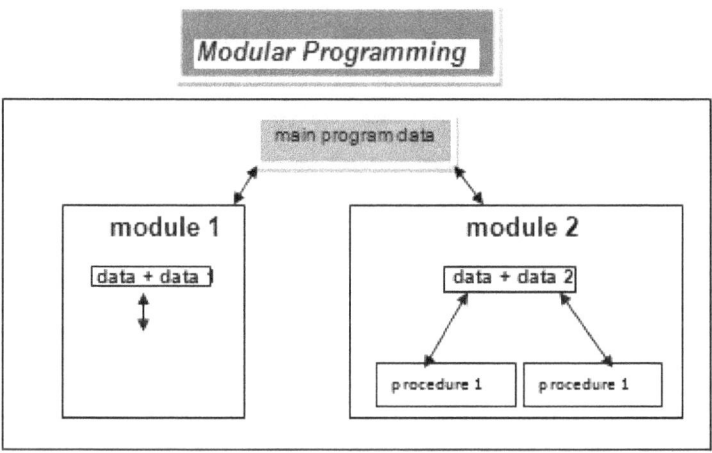

In this fast processing and ongoing demands for better results we are use to the technologies because it makes our life simpler and easier but you know the programs or software like Microsoft Word, Microsoft Excel, MS-Paint, Word-Pad, Notepad, PowerPoint , even a simple calculator needs to be run by number of codes which is created by a programmer in form of small-small programs.

these programs build by the programmers contains thousands or millions of lines of code, which is a difficult task itself. one can imagine , how difficult it is to write a lot of codes and how hard it is to prepare. How do find out the mistakes in such a long code? how to add and remove some codes in the big program? and how to handle the problem?

To solve this problem, the programmers have to use the concept of modular programming. Actually, we follow this technique when our programs become large, we divided the large programs into small pieces called **modules**. By making a small block of statements inside the module. We write many lines of code inside our module to do a particular task, simply like to add two numbers, to find the area of geometrical objects, and to do various complex algorithms. We can test each module separately and we can easily debug the program.

*Definition*

*Modular programming is an approach of programming in which a large program is divided into separate independent units called modules.*

**Module** refers to the block of statements or set of instructions to perform specific tasks in the program. It is also known as 'Procedure'. To build the complete software programmers have to make many separate modules and finally these modules combined together.

## A modular program consist of main module and sub-module.

1. Main module : Modular Programming structure consists of many modules, the program entry point is a module, which is located at the top of the order modules. This top level module is called main module. The main module is the controlling section of a

**modular programming**.

2. Sub- module : Sub- module is a program which is written under the main module. A modular program may have one or more than one sub- module. It is called sub- program. Q-basic is also known as modular programming language because it allows the user to divide program into manageable and functional modules or blocks with the help of **sub procedure and function procedure**.

# Advantages of Modular Programming

There are many advantages of modular programming, some of them are given below.

- It's easy to understand and manage the program's code.
- In different modules of the same program, different programmers can be able to work at the same time, for that reason within a short period of time perfect program can be prepared.
- Once the module is ready, the module can be repeatedly used in anywhere the program. Due to this time and computer memory will be saved.
- Each module can be tested by running it separately, due to this programmers can find the faults in the program and debug them.
- Changing something in the program will be quick and easy.

## Procedure

The procedure is a set of instructions that is build to perform a specific task in the program. It is also known as a sub-program. Each procedure has its own unique name which is also called procedure name. We can use this procedure in any part of the program by calling them. In QBASIC there are two types of procedures.

1. **SUB** Procedure
2. **FUNCTION** Procedure

**Sub Procedure** : A sub procedure is a small manageable and functional part of a program that performs specific tasks and does not return any value to the calling module. A sub program is written with SUB....END SUB statements.

**Some important features of sub procedure are as follows:**

- It does not return any value.
- Sub procedure name can't be used as variable.
- Arguments can be passed to the sun program by reference or value.

**Function Procedure** :

A function procedure is small manageable and functional part of a program that performs the specific tasks and returns a single value to the main program or calling module. A function is written with FUNCTION.......END FUNCTION statement.

## Some important features of function procedure are as follows:

- It returns a value.
- Function procedure name has type declaration sign.
- Arguments can be passed to the sub-program by reference or by value.

## Arguments

The constant or variables enclosed in the parentheses of procedure call statement and that are supplied to the procedure are known as arguments. The argument can be passed to a procedure either by reference or by value method.

**Formal and Actual Parameter:** Formal parameters are used to specify or declare the type of data to be passed to the procedures either by sub or function procedure.

*Parameters*

Variables in sub procedure declaration which accept data or variables passed to them from the calling module are known as parameters. It is also known as formal parameter.

**Local and Global variable :** A variable which is defined in a module ans is not accessible to any other modules is known as local variable. A variable in main module which can be accessed from any module or procedure of a program is known as global variable.

## Exercise

---

## Write A Program Using Sub...End To Display Temperature In Celsius Of A Temperature Input In Fahrenheit. (Hint: Celsius =5 (Fahrenheit-32)/9).

```
DECLARE SUB Temperature (F)
CLS
Input"Enter the temperature in Fahrenheit"; F
CALL Temperature (F)
END
SUB Temperature (F)
Temperature in Celsius= (5(f-32)/9)
Print"The temperature in Celsius"; Temperature in Celsius
END SUB
```

**Write a program to define a sub procedure to display simple interest where users input the required data in the main module.**

```
DECLARE SUB Interest (P, T, R)
CLS
Input"Enter the principle"; P
Input"Enter the time"; T
Input"Enter the rate"; R
CALL Interest (P, T, R)
END
SUB Interest (P, T, R)
I= (P*T*R)/100
Print"The simple interest is"; I
END SUB
```

## Write a program to declare a sub procedure to display the perimeter of rectangle.

```
DECLARE SUB Area (L, B)
CLS
Input "Enter the length"; L
Input "Enter the breadth"; B
CALL Area (L, B)
END
SUB Area (L, B)
A = (2*(L+B))
Print "The area of rectangle is"; A
END SUB
```

## Write a program using FUNCTION...END FUNCTION statement to calculate area of a rectangle.

```
DECLARE FUNCTION AREA (L, B)
CLS
Input "Enter the length"; L
Input "Enter the breadth"; B
Print "The area is"; AREA (L, B)
END

FUNCTION AREA (L, B)
```

```
AREA= L*B
END FUNCTION
```

## WAP to input length and find out area of square.

```
DECLARE SUB Area (1)
CLS
INPUT "Enter the length";l
CALL Area (1)
END
SUB Area (1)
A = 1^ 2
PRINT" Area of square"; A
END SUB
```

# LIBRARY FUNCTION IN QBASIC

A function is a built-in formula or a ready-made program that helps us to perform a certain task such as mathematical, financial, logical, etc.

A function manipulates data passes to it and returns either a string or a numeric value. There are two types of functions in QBASIC Programming.

1.  **User-defined function**
2.  **Built-in function**

**1. User-defined function:**
It is created by the programmer to perform the operations as per the requirements. It can be a numeric or string function.

**2. Built-in function:**

It is a pre-defined program which is provided by QBASIC to perform some task easily. It gives many more built-in functions for manipulating strings, numbers. It makes our work easy. It is also known as Library functions. There are two types of built in function:

## Mathematical Functions

1. SQR : It calculate and return the square root of non-negative number

2. MOD : It returns reminder, when one number is divide by another number.

3. INT : It returns an integer of a given number.

4. CINT : It returns nearest rounding numeric value from -32768 to 32767 as argument.

5. SGN : It returns the sign of numeric value.

6. SIN : It returns the sign value of given number.

7. COS : It is used to obtain the cosine value of a number.

8. TAN : It returns the tangent of a number.

9. ABS : It returns corresponding positive value.

## String Functions

1. UCASE$ : It converts string values to uppercase.

2. LCASE$ : It converts string values to lowercase.

3. LEFT$ : It extract and return the numbers of characters from the left of a string.

4. RIGHT$ : It extract and return the numbers of characters from the right of a string.

5. MID$ : It is used to pick up the required strings from the string.

6. LTRIM$ : It is used to remove the spaces from the left of the string.

7. RTRIM$ : it is used to remove the spaces from the right of the string.

8. VAL : If both strings are started with numeric value. This function can perform mathematical calculations among them.

9. ASC : It returns ASCII value of a character.

10. CHR$ : It returns character value of given ASCII code.

11. STR$ : It converts numeric value to string value, which cannot be used for mathematical calculation.
12. SPACE$ : It is used to put blank space.

13. TAB : It is used to put Tab.

14. DATE$ : It returns the current date.

15. TIME$ : It returns the current time.

16. LEN : It returns the length of a given string.

17. STRING$ : It returns a string of a specified length made up of a repeating character.

ΔΔΔ

# NUMERICAL METHODS-II

## Trapezoidal Rule

In Calculus, "Trapezoidal Rule" is one of the important integration rules. The name trapezoidal is because when the area under the curve is evaluated, then the total area is divided into small trapezoids instead of rectangles. This rule is used for approximating the definite integrals where it uses the linear approximations of the functions.

Trapezoidal Rule is a rule that evaluates the area under the curves by dividing the total area into smaller trapezoids rather than using rectangles. This integration works by approximating the region under the graph of a function as a trapezoid, and it calculates the area. This rule takes the average of the left and the right sum.

The Trapezoidal Rule does not give accurate value as Simpson's Rule when the underlying function is smooth. It is because Simpson's Rule uses the quadratic approximation instead of linear approximation. Both Simpson's Rule and Trapezoidal Rule give the approximation value, but Simpson's Rule results in even more accurate approximation value of the integrals.

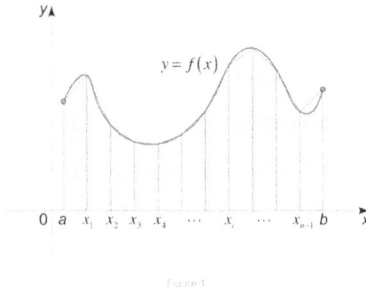

figure 1

The bounding curve in the segment is considered to be a straight line, as shown in the figure, as a result the enclosed area becomes a trapezium. The area of each small trapezium is added to give the value of the integral.

## Formula For Trapezoidal Rule

Let f(x) be a continuous function on the interval [a, b]. Now divide the intervals [a, b] into n equal subintervals with each of width,

$$\Delta x = (b-a)/n,$$

Such that $a = x_0 < x_1 < x_2 < x_3 < ..... < x_n = b$

Then the Trapezoidal Rule formula for area approximating the definite integral ∫ab f(x)dx is given by:

$$\int_a^b f(x)dx \approx T_n = \frac{\Delta x}{2}[f(x_0) + 2f(x_1) + 2f(x_2) + ....2f(x_{n-1}) + f(x_n)]$$

Where, $x_i = a + i\Delta x$

If $n \to \infty$, R.H.S of the expression approaches the definite integral ∫ ab f(x)dx .

## ❖ Guidelines for writing the program

- Given a function $f(x)$

- Get Inputs (the limits $a$ and $b$, no. of even subintervals $n$)

- Set $h = (a + b)/n$

- Evaluate $f(a)$ and $f(b)$

- Initialize $sum$

- Run the loop (choose the loop counters carefully) to find $sum = sum + f(a + counter \cdot h)$

- Put the values in the formula for $I$

- Print $I$

## ❖ Program for trapezoidal rule in q-basic

## Program

**10 CLS**
**20 REM program for trapezoidal value**
**30 INPUT " enter number of data "; n**

```
40 FOR i = 1 TO n
   50 INPUT x(i), y(i)
60 NEXT i
70 h = x(2) - x(1)
80 FOR i = 2 TO n - 1
   90 sum = sum + y(i)
100 NEXT i
110 in = h * (y(1) + 2 * sum + y(n)) / 2
120 PRINT " i = "; i, t
130 END
```

note*** area of a trapezoid is

$$Area = (h/2) [y_0 + 2 (y_1 + y_2 + y_3 + ..... + y_{n-1}) + y_n]$$

### ❖ wap to calculate value of sin(x)

Sin x is a series of sin function of trigonometry; it can expand up to infinite number of term. Through this series, we can find out value of sin x at any radian value of sin x graph.

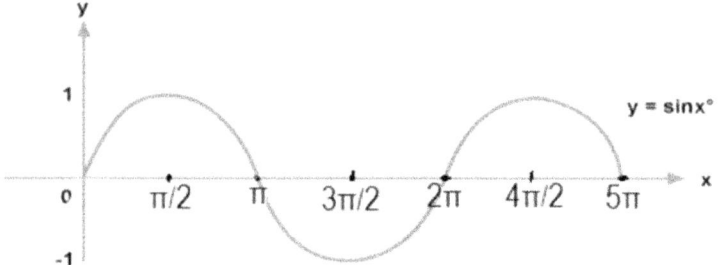

## Sin X Series:

$$\sin(x) = \sum_{k=0}^{\infty} \frac{(-1)^k}{(2k+1)!} x^{2k+1} = x - \frac{x^3}{3!} + \frac{x^5}{5!} - \cdots$$

algorithim

1. First the computer reads the value of $x$ and limit from the user.
2. Now convert $x$ to radian value x=x*(3.1415\180)
3. Then using for loop the value of $\sin(x)$ is calculated.
4. Finally the value of $\sin(x)$ is printed.

## ◆ Program For Sin(X) Series

```
cls
input "enter angle is degree " ; angle
x = (3.146 + angle ) / 180
term = x : i = 1
sum = term
while ABS (term) < .0001
new term = ((-1)*term/(2*(I + 1 ))*(2*i);sum = sum + new term
term = new term : I = I + 1
wend
print sum
end
```

## Palindrome

A palindrome is a word, number, phrase, or other sequence of symbols that reads the same backwards as forwards, such as the words *madam* or *racecar*, bob, noon, redder .

Palindrome numbers can be considered in numeral systems other than decimal. For example, the binary palindrome numbers are those with the binary representations: 0, 1, 11, 101, 111, 1001, 1111, 10001, 10101, 11011, 11111, 10000,1991.

❖ QBasic Check if number is Palindrome using for loop**Program**

**Cls**

**Rem**

**Input " enter the string "; a$**

**L = len(a$)**

**For i = 1 to l / 2**

**if mid$(a$, i, 1) <> mid$(a$, l - 1 + 1) then print " string "; a$; "is not "**

**Next i**

**Print a$; " is a palindrome"**

**End**

**program with its output**

# Lagrange's Interpolation Formula

The Newton's forward and backward interpolation formulae can be used only when the values of $x$ are at equidistant.

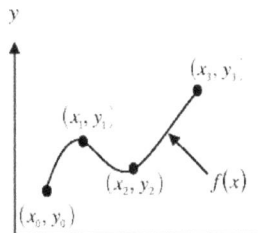

If the values of $x$ are at equidistant or not at equidistant, we use Lagrange's interpolation formula.

Let $y = f(x)$ be a function such that

$f(x)$ takes the values $y_0$, $y_1$, $y_2$,......., $y_n$ corresponding to $x = x_0$, $x_1$, $x_2$ ..., $x_n$ That is $y_i = f(x_i)$, $i = 0,1,2,...,n$ . Now, there are $(n + 1)$ paired values $(x_i, y_i)$, $i = 0, 1, 2, ..., n$ and hence $f(x)$ can be represented by a polynomial function of degree n in x.

Then the Lagrange's formula is

$$y = f(x) = \frac{(x-x_1)(x-x_2)...(x-x_n)}{(x_0-x_1)(x_0-x_2)...(x_0-x_n)}y_0 + \frac{(x-x_0)(x-x_2)...(x-x_n)}{(x_1-x_0)(x_1-x_2)...(x_1-x_n)}y_1$$
$$+...+ \frac{(x-x_0)(x-x_1)...(x-x_{n-1})}{(x_n-x_0)(x_n-x_1)...(x_n-x_{n-1})}y_n$$

◆ Algorithm: Lagrange Interpolation Method

**1. Start**

**2. Read number of data (n)**

**3. Read data Xi and Yi for i=1 ton n**

**4. Read value of independent variables say xp**

whose corresponding value of dependent say yp is to be determined.

5. Initialize: yp = 0

6. For i = 1 to n

   Set p = 1

   For j =1 to n

   If i ≠ j then

   Calculate p = p * (xp - Xj)/(Xi - Xj)

   End If

   Next j

   Calculate yp = yp + p * Yi

   Next j

6. Display value of yp as interpolated value.

7. Stop

```
File  Edit  View  Search  Run  Options

CLS
REM program for langrange method
INPUT "enter number of data "; n
FOR i = 1 TO n
    INPUT x(i), y(j)
NEXT i
INPUT " enter the value of x "; x
FOR j = 1 TO n
    p = 1
    FOR j = 1 TO n
        IF i <> j THEN
            p = p * (xp - Xj) / (Xi - Xj)
        END IF
    NEXT j
    yp = yp + p * y(i)
NEXT j
PRINT "y = "; y
END
```

```
enter number of data ? 5
? 1
? 2
? 3
? 4
? 8
 enter the value of x ? 2
y =  0
```

# Simpson's Rule

**Simpson's rule** is one of the numerical methods which is used to evaluate the definite integral. Usually, to find the definite integral, we use the fundamental theorem of calculus, where we have to apply the ant derivative techniques of integration. However, sometimes, it isn't easy to find the ant derivative of an integral, like in Scientific Experiments, where the function has to be determined from the observed readings. Therefore, numerical methods are used to approximate the integral in such conditions. Other numerical methods used are trapezoidal rule, midpoint rule, left or right approximation using Riemann sums. Here, we will discuss Simpson's rule formula, 1/3 rule, 3/8 rule .

$$\int_a^b f(x)\, dx \approx \frac{b-a}{6} \left[ f(a) + 4f\left(\frac{a+b}{2}\right) + f(b) \right]$$

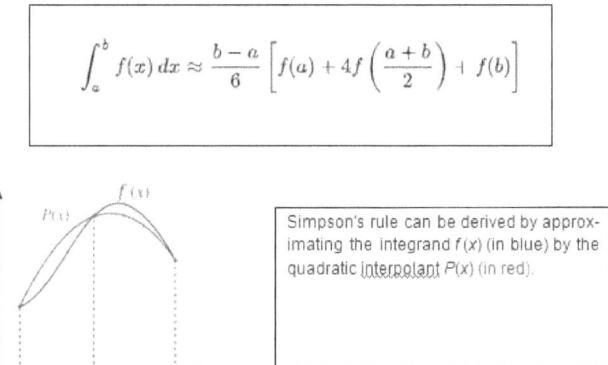

Simpson's rule can be derived by approximating the integrand $f(x)$ (in blue) by the quadratic interpolant $P(x)$ (in red).

## *Simpson's 1/3 Rule*

Simpson's 1/3rd rule is an extension of the trapezoidal rule in which the integrand is approximated by a second-order polynomial. Simpson rule can be derived from the various way using Newton's divided difference polynomial, Lagrange polynomial and the method of coefficients. Simpson's 1/3 rule is defined by:

$$\int_a^b f(x)\,dx = h/3\,[(y_0 + y_n) + 4(y_1 + y_3 + y_5 + \ldots + y_{n-1}) + 2(y_2 + y_4 + y_6 + \ldots + y_{n-2})]$$

This rule is known as Simpson's **One-third rule**.

### ❖ Simpson's ⅓ Rule for Integration

We can get a quick approximation for definite integrals when we divide a small interval [a, b] into two parts. Therefore, after dividing the interval, we get;

$x_0 = a,\ x_1 = a + b,\ x_2 = b$

Hence, we can write the approximation as;

$\int_a^b f(x)\,dx \approx S_2 = h/3[f(x_0) + 4f(x_1) + f(x_2)]$

$S_2 = h/3\,[f(a) + 4\,f((a+b)/2) + f(b)]$

Where $h = (b - a)/2$

This is the Simpson's ⅓ rule for integration.

### ❖ Simpson's 3/8 Rule

Another method of numerical integration is called "Simpson's 3/8 rule". It is completely based on the cubic interpolation rather than the quadratic interpolation. Simpson's 3/8 or three-eight rule is given by:

$$\int_a^b f(x)\, dx = 3h/8\, [(y_0 + y_n) + 3(y_1 + y_2 + y_4 + y_5 + \ldots + y_{n-1}) + 2(y_3 + y_6 + y_9 + \ldots + y_{n-3})]$$

This rule is more accurate than the standard method, as it uses one more functional value. For 3/8 rule, the composite Simpson's 3/8 rule also exists which is similar to the generalized form.

*The 3/8 rule is known as Simpson's second rule of integration.*

```
 File  Edit  View  Search  Run  Options

10 CLS
20 REM " **************** Simpson's 3/8rd Rule ****************"
30 INPUT " No. of Discrete Data Points n"; n
40 IF n MOD 3 <> 0 THEN PRINT " n Should be Multiple of 3": GOTO 30
50 INPUT "limits of integration a,b"; a, b
60 h = (b - a) / (n - 1)
70 FOR i = 1 TO n
80  x(i) = a + (i - 1) * h
90  PRINT "x(i) for i = "; i; "is"; x(i)
100  INPUT "Value of y for x(i) is"; y(i)
110 NEXT i
120 S1 = 0
130 S3 = 0
140 FOR i = 2 TO n - 1
150  IF i MOD 3 = 0 THEN S3 = S3 + y(i) ELSE S1 = S1 + y(i)
160 NEXT i
170 IM = (3 * h * (y(1) + y(n) + 3 * S1 + 2 * S3)) / 8
180 PRINT "Integral is "; IM
190 END
```

## ❖ SIMPSON'S RULE ERROR

Although in Simpson's rule method we get a more accurate approximation for definite integral, still the error occurs which is defined when n = 2;

$$-(1/90)[(b-a)/2]^5 f^{(4)}(\xi)$$

Where $\xi$ is some number between a and b.

❖ *Runge–Kutta method*

As we know, Taylor's series is a numerical method used for solving differential equations and is limited by the work to be done in finding the derivatives of the higher-order. To overcome this, we can use a new category of numerical methods called **Runge-Kutta methods** to solve differential equations. These will give us higher accuracy without performing more calculations.

These methods coordinate with the solution of Talor's series up to the term in hr, where r varies from method to method, representing the order of that method. One of the most significant advantages of Runge-Kutaa formulae is that it requires the function's values at some specified points.

Before learning about the **Runge-Kutta RK4 method**, let's have a look at the formulas of the first, second and third-order Runge-Kutta methods.

Consider an ordinary differential equation of the form $dy/dx = f(x, y)$ with initial condition $y(x_0) = y_0$. For this, we can define the formulas for Runge-Kutta methods as follows.

❖ **1st Order Runge-Kutta method**

$y_1 = y_0 + hf(x_0, y_0) = y_0 + hy'_0$ {since $y' = f(x, y)$}
This formula is same as the Euler's method

❖ **2nd Order Runge-Kutta method**

$y_1 = y_0 + (1/2)(k_1 + k_2)$
Here,
$k_1 = hf(x_0, y_0)$
$k_2 = hf(x_0 + h, y_0 + k_1)$

❖ **3rd Order Runge-Kutta method**

$y_1 = y_0 + (\tfrac{1}{6})(k_1 + 4k_2 + k_3)$

Here,

$k_1 = hf(x_0, y_0)$

$k_2 = hf[x_0 + (\tfrac{1}{2})h, y_0 + (\tfrac{1}{2})k_1]$

$k_3 = hf(x_0 + h, y_0 + k^1)$ such that $k^1 = hf(x_0 + h, y_0 + k_1)$

❖ *Fourth Order RK Method*

The most commonly used Runge Kutta method to find the solution of a differential equation is the RK4 method, i.e., the fourth-order Runge-Kutta method. The Runge-Kutta method provides the approximate value of y for a given point x. Only the first order ODEs can be solved using the Runge Kutta RK4 method.

❖ **Runge-Kutta Fourth Order Method Formula**

The formula for the fourth-order Runge-Kutta method is given by:

$y_1 = y_0 + (\tfrac{1}{6})(k_1 + 2k_2 + 2k_3 + k_4)$

Here,

$$k_1 = hf(x_0, y_0)$$
$$k_2 = hf[x_0 + (\tfrac{1}{2})h, y_0 + (\tfrac{1}{2})k_1]$$
$$k_3 = hf[x_0 + (\tfrac{1}{2})h, y_0 + (\tfrac{1}{2})k_2]$$
$$k_4 = hf(x_0 + h, y_0 + k_3)$$

## ❖ Multiplication Of Matrices

## Program -

CLS

REM multiplication of matrices

DIM a(10, 10), b(10, 10), c(10, 10)

INPUT " enter order of 1 st matrix "; m, n

INPUT " enter order of 2nd matrices "; p, q

IF (n <> p) THEN PRINT " matrix multiplication is not possible ": END

PRINT " enter elements of matrix a "

FOR i = 1 TO m

   FOR j = 1 TO n

      INPUT a(i, j)

   NEXT j

NEXT i

PRINT " enter elements of matrix b "

FOR i = 0 TO p

   FOR j = 0 TO q

      INPUT b(i, j)

   NEXT j

   FOR j = 1 TO q

      c(i, j) = 0

   NEXT j

NEXT i

FOR i = 1 TO m

   FOR j = 1 TO q

      c(i, j) = 0

      FOR k = 1 TO p

         c(i, j) = c(i, j) + a(i, k) * b(k, j)

      NEXT k

   NEXT j

NEXT i

**PRINT " product of matrices "**

**FOR i = 1 TO m**

  **FOR j = 1 TO q**

    **PRINT " "; c(i, j)**

  **NEXT j**

**NEXT i**

**END**

# ❖ Practical Based Programming

## Bisection Method -

The bisection method is an approximation method to find the roots of the given equation by repeatedly dividing the interval. This method will divide the interval until the resulting interval is found, which is extremely small.

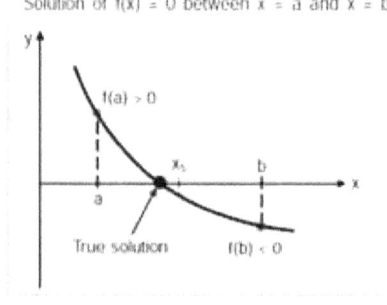

Solution of f(x) = 0 between x = a and x = b

Let us consider a continuous function "f" which is defined on the closed interval [a, b], is given with f(a) and f(b) of different signs. Then by intermediate theorem, there exists a point x belong to (a, b) for which f(x) = 0.

Bisection Method Algorithm

Follow the below procedure to get the

solution for the continuous function:

For any continuous function f(x),

1. Find two points, say a and b such that a < b and f(a)* f(b) < 0

2. Find the midpoint of a and b, say "t"

3. t is the root of the given function if f(t) = 0; else follow the next step

4. Divide the interval [a, b] – If f(t)*f(a) <0, there exist a root between t and a

– else if f(t) *f (b) < 0, there exist a root between t and b

5. Repeat above three steps until f(t) = 0.

The bisection method is an approximation method to find the roots of the given equation by repeatedly dividing the interval. This method will divide the interval until the resulting interval is found, which is extremely small.

*************************************************************************************

Problem: Write a program in Q-basic to solve the equation below, by using bisection method:

F ( x) = x ^2 -5x+6 , [0,1] , e = 0.001

*********************************************************************************CLS

REM program for bisection method

deffna(x) = x ^ x - 5 * x + 6

INPUT " enter initial gauss values "; x0, x1

INPUT " permissible error "; e

f0 = fna(x0)

f1 = fna(x1)

IF f0 * f1 > 0 THEN PRINT " initial value "; x0, x1

f0 = fna(x0)

f1 = fna(x1)

IF f0 * f1 > 0 THEN PRINT " initial value gauss wrong "

x2 = (x1 + x0) / 2

f2 = fna(x2)

IF f0 * f1 > 0 THEN x0 = x2: ELSE x1 = x2: f1 = f2

IF ABS(x0 - x1) < e THEN PRINT " root is "; (x0 + x1) / 2: END

***********************************************************************************

output

enter initial gauss value ? 2,2

permissible error ? 0.001

root is 2

*-*-*-*-*-*-**-*-*-*-*-*-*-*-*-*-*-*-*-*-*-*-*-*-*-*-*-*-*-*-*-*-*-*-

```
CLS
REM program for bisection method
deffna(x) = x ^ x - 5 * x + 6
INPUT " enter initial gauss values "; x0, x1
INPUT " permissible error "; e
f0 = fna(x0)
f1 = fna(x1)
IF f0 * f1 > 0 THEN PRINT " initial value "; x0, x1
f0 = fna(x0)
f1 = fna(x1)
IF f0 * f1 > 0 THEN PRINT " initial value gauss wrong "
x2 = (x1 + x0) / 2
f2 = fna(x2)
IF f0 * f1 > 0 THEN x0 = x2: ELSE x1 = x2: f1 = f2
IF ABS(x0 - x1) < e THEN PRINT " root is "; (x0 + x1) / 2: END
```

output

```
enter initial gauss values ? 2,2
permissible error ? 0.001
root is 2
```

********************************************************************************

# False Position Method (Or) Regula Falsi Method

an ancient method of solving an equation in one variable is the false position method (method of false position) or regula falsi method.

In simple words, the method is described as the trial

and error approach of using "false" or "test" values for the variable and then altering the test value according to the result . This is sometimes also referred to as "guess and check".

The formulas for the approximation of roots of the equation by false positive method are given below:

x1 = [af(b) – bf(a)]/ [f(b) – f(a)]; where a < b

x2 = [af(x1) – x1f(a)]/ [f(x1) – f(a)]

Consider an equation f(x) = 0, which contains only one variable, i.e. x. To find the real root of the equation f(x) = 0, we consider a sufficiently small interval (a, b) where a < b such that f(a) and f(b) will have opposite signs. According to the intermediate value theorem, this implies a root lies between a and b.

Also, the curve y = f(x) will meet the x-axis at a certain point between A[a, f(a)] and B[b, f(b)].

Now, the equation of the chord joining A[a, f(a)] and B[b, f(b)] is given by:

$$y - f(a) = \frac{f(b) - f(a)}{(b - a)} \cdot (x - a)$$

Let y = 0 be the point of intersection of the chord equation (given above) with the x-axis. Then,

$$-f(a) = \frac{f(b) - f(a)}{(b - a)} \cdot (x - a)$$

This can be simplified as :-

$$\frac{f(a)(b-a)}{f(b)-f(a)} = x - a$$

$$\frac{af(a)-bf(a)}{f(b)-f(a)} + a = x$$

$$\Rightarrow x = \frac{af(a)-bf(a)+af(b)-af(a)}{f(b)-f(a)}$$

$$\Rightarrow x = \frac{af(b)-bf(a)}{f(b)-f(a)}$$

Thus, the first approximation is -

x1 = [af(b) – bf(a)]/ [f(b) – f(a)] .

Also, x1 is the root of f(x) if f(x1) = 0. If f(x1) ≠ 0 and if f(x1) and f(a) have opposite signs, then we can write the second approximation as:

x2 = [af(x1) – x1f(a)]/ [f(x1) – f(a)],

Similarly, we can estimate x3, x4, x5, and so on.
Geometrical representation of the roots of the equation f(x) = 0 can be shown as:

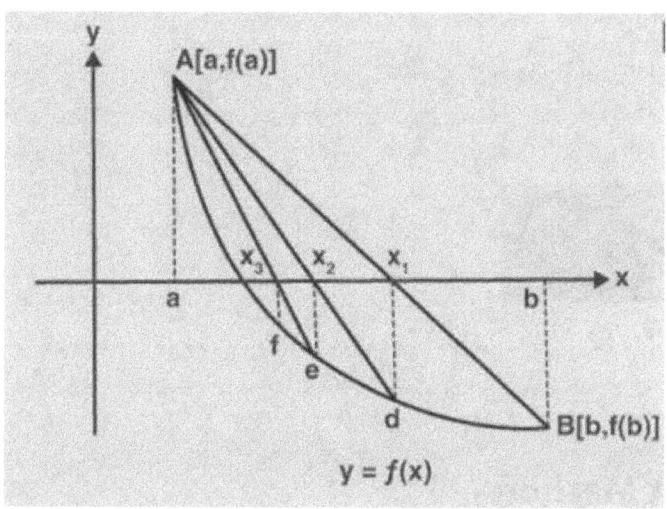

$y = f(x)$

\*\*\*\*\*\*\*\*\*\*\*\*\*\*\*\*\*\*\*\*\*\*\*\*\*\*\*\*\*\*\*\*\*\*\*\*\*\*\*\*\*\*\*\*\*\*\*\*\*\*\*\*\*\*\*\*\*\*\*\*\*\*\*\*\*\*\*\*\*\*\*\*\*\*\*\*\*\*\*\*\*\*\*

Problem: Write the program in Q-basic to find the root of the function below by using false position method:

f ( x) = x log( x) - 1 , [1,2] , e = 0.0001
\*\*\*\*\*\*\*\*\*\*\*\*\*\*\*\*\*\*\*\*\*\*\*\*\*\*\*\*\*\*\*\*\*\*\*\*\*\*\*\*\*\*\*\*\*\*\*\*\*\*\*\*\*\*\*\*\*\*\*\*\*\*\*\*\*\*\*\*\*\*\*\*\*\*\*CLS

```
deffnf(x) = xlOG(x) - 1
READ a, b, e
DATA 1,2,0.0001
c0 = bf1 = fnf(a): f2 = fnf(b)
5 c = (a * f2 - b * f1) / (f2 - f1)
PRINT c
f3 = fnf(c)
IF f1 * f3 = 0 THEN 25
IF f2 * f3 = 0 THEN 25
IF f1 * f3 < 0 THEN 15
a = c: f1 = f3
GOTO 20
```

```
15 b = c: f2 = f3
20 IF ABS(c - c0) < e THEN 25
c0 = c
GOTO 5
25 PRINT "the root is:", c
END
```

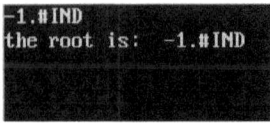

*^*^*^*^*^*^*^*^*^*^*^*^*^*^*^*^**^*^*^*^*^*^*^*^*^*^*^*^*^*^*

# Secant Method -

It is a root-finding procedure in numerical analysis that uses a series of roots of secant lines to better approximate a root of a function. The tangent line to the curve of y = f(x) with the point of tangency (x0, f(x0) was used in Newton's approach. The graph of the tangent line about x = α is essentially the same as the graph of y = f(x) when x0 ≈ α. The root of the tangent line was used to approximate α.

Consider employing an approximating line based on 'interpolation'. Let's pretend we have two root estimations of root α, say, x0 and x1. Then, we have a linear function

q(x) = a0 + a1x

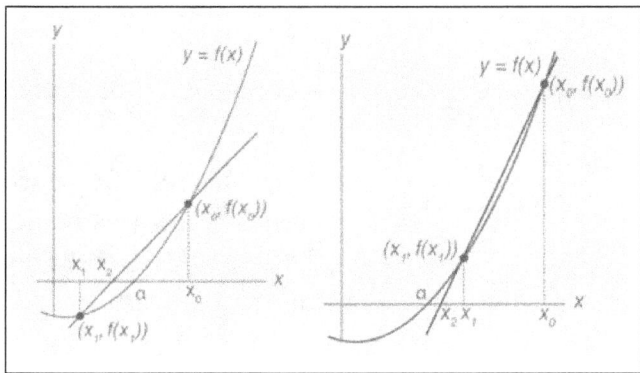

using q(x0) = f (x0), q(x1) = f (x1).

This line is also known as a secant line. Its formula is as follows:

$$q(x) = \frac{(x_1 - x)f(x_0) + (x - x_0)f(x_1)}{x_1 - x_0}$$

The linear equation q(x) = 0 is now solved, with the root denoted by x2. This results in

$$x_2 = x_1 - f(x_1) \cdot \frac{x_1 - x_0}{f(x_1) - f(x_0)}$$

Let the above form be equation (1)

The procedure can now be repeated. Employ x1 and x2 to create a new secant line, and then use the root of that line to approximate α;...

**Secant Method Steps**

The secant method procedures are given below using equation (1).

Step 1: Initialization

x0 and x1 of α are taken as initial guesses.

Step 2: Iteration

In the case of n = 1, 2, 3, ...,

$$x_{n+1} = x_n - f(x_n) \cdot \frac{x_n - x_{n-1}}{f(x_n) - f(x_{n-1})}$$ until a specific criterion for termination has been met (i.e., The desired accuracy of the answer or the maximum number of iterations has been attained).

**Secant Method Convergence**

If the initial values x0 and x1 are close enough to the root, the secant method iterates xn and converges to a root of function f. The order of convergence is given by φ, where

$$\varphi = \frac{1 + \sqrt{5}}{2} \approx 1.618,$$

Which is the golden ratio.

The convergence is particularly superlinear, but not really quadratic. This solution is only valid under certain technical requirements, such as f being two times continuously differentiable and the root being simple in the question (i.e., having multiplicity 1).

There is no certainty that the secant method will converge if the beginning values are not close enough to the root. For instance, if the function f is differentiable on the interval [x0, x1], and there is a point on the interval where f' =0, the algorithm may not converge.

**advantages of secant method:**

1. It converges quicker than a linear rate, making it more convergent than the bisection method.
2. It does not necessitate the usage of the function's derivative,

which is not available in a number of applications.

3. Unlike Newton's technique, which requires two function evaluations in every iteration, it only requires one.

**Drawbacks of secant method:**

The secant method may not converge.

The computed iterates have no guaranteed error bounds.

If $f0(\alpha) = 0$, it is likely to be challenging. This means that when x = $\alpha$, the x-axis is tangent to the graph of $y = f(x)$.

Newton's approach is more easily generalized to new ways for solving nonlinear simultaneous systems of equations.

*^*^*^*^*^**^*^*^*^*^*^*^*^*^*^*^*^*^*^*^*^*^*^*^*^*^*^**^*^*

Problem: Write a program in Q-basic by using secant method to find the root of:

F ( X) = X 3 – 3X + 2 , [−2.4,−2.6] , E = 0.005

***********************************************************************

```
CLS
DEFFNF(X) = X ^ 3 - 3 * X + 2
READ A, B, E
DATA -2.4,-2.6,0.005
F1 = FNF(A)
10 F2 = FNF(B)
C = (A * F2 - B * F1) / (F2 - F1)
PRINT C
F3 = FNF(C)
IF ABS(A - B) < E THEN 25
A = B: B = C: F1 = F2
GOTO 10
25 PRINT "THE ROOT IS:", C
END
```

***********************************************************************

# Lagrange Interpolating Polynomial

It is the unique polynomial of lowest degree that interpolates a given set of data.

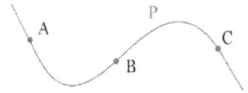

lagrange interpolation polynomial through any point

## Lagrange Interpolation Formula

If you are having 2 points with coordinates (x1,y1) and (x2,y2), the Lagrange Interpolation will be:

$$y - y1 = (y2 - y1)/(x2-x1) * (x-x1)$$

## Lagrange Interpolation Properties

If G is a finite order m group, then the order of any aG divides the order of G, and am = e.

If finite group G's order is a prime order, it has no appropriate subgroups.

*A cyclic group is a group of prime order (the order has only two divisors).*

\*\*\*\*\*\*\*\*\*\*\*\*\*\*\*\*\*\*\*\*\*\*\*\*\*\*\*\*\*\*\*\*\*\*\*\*\*\*\*\*\*\*\*\*\*\*\*\*\*\*\*\*\*\*\*\*\*\*\*\*\*\*\*\*\*\*\*\*\*\*

Problem: Write a program to find the interpolated value for x = 3 , using Lagrangian Polynomial, from the following data.

| X | 3.2 | 2.7 | 1 | 4.8 |
|------|------|------|------|------|
| F(x) | 22 | 17.8 | 14.2 | 38.3 |

\*\*\*\*\*\*\*\*\*\*\*\*\*\*\*\*\*\*\*\*\*\*\*\*\*\*\*\*\*\*\*\*\*\*\*\*\*\*\*\*\*\*\*\*\*\*\*\*\*\*\*\*\*\*\*\*\*\*\*\*\*\*\*\*\*\*\*\*\*\*

```
REM "Lagrange Interpolation"
CLS
DIM x(100), y(100) I
```

```
NPUT "No. of pairs"; n
 INPUT "x="; x
FOR k = 0 TO n - 1
READ x(k), y(k)
NEXT k
DATA 3.2,22,2.7,17.8,1,14.2,4.8,38.3
sum = 0
FOR i = 0 TO n - 1
 prod = 1
FOR k = 0 TO n - 1
IF i = k THEN
5 prod = prod * (x - x(k)) / (x(i) - x(k)) 5
NEXT k sum = sum + prod * y(i)
NEXT i
PRINT "x="; x; "y="; sum
 END
        --------*************------------
```

*No. of Pairs? 4 X=? 3 X=3 y=20.21196*


*************************************************************************


# Newton - Raphson Method:

The Newton Raphson Method is referred to as one of the most commonly used techniques for finding the roots of given equations. It can be efficiently generalised to find solutions to a system of equations. Moreover, we can show that when we approach the root, the method is quadratically convergent. In this article, you will learn how to use the Newton Raphson method to find the roots or solutions of a given equation, and the geometric interpretation of this method.

### Newton Raphson Method Formula

Let x0 be the approximate root of f(x) = 0 and let x1 = x0 + h be the correct root. Then f(x1) = 0

⇒ f(x0 + h) = 0....(1)

By expanding the above equation using Taylor's theorem, we get:

f(x0) + hf1(x0) + ... = 0

⇒ h = -f(x0) /f'(x0)

Therefore, x1 = x0 – f(x0)/ f'(x0)

Now, x1 is the better approximation than x0.

Similarly, the successive approximations x2, x3, ...., xn+1 are given by

$$x_{n+1} = x_n - \frac{f(x_n)}{f'(x_n)}$$

This is called Newton Raphson formula. Other formulas include the following:

| | |
|---|---|
| Newton's Iterative Formula to Find b<sup>th</sup> Root of a Positive Real Number a | The iterative formula is given by: $$x_{n+1} = \frac{1}{b}\left[(b-1)x_n + \frac{a}{x_n^{b-1}}\right]$$ |
| Newton's Iterative Formula to Find a Reciprocal of a Number N | The iterative formula is given by: $x_{i+1} = x_i(2 - x_i N)$ |

## Geometrical Interpretation of Newton Raphson Formula

The geometric meaning of Newton's Raphson method is that a tangent is drawn at the point [x0, f(x0)] to the curve y = f(x).

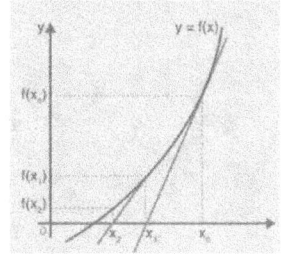

It cuts the x-axis at x1, which will be a better approximation of the root. Now, drawing another tangent at [x1, f(x1)], which cuts the x-axis at x2, which is a still better approximation and the process can be continued till the desired accuracy is achieved.

## Convergence of Newton Raphson Method

The order of convergence of Newton Raphson method is 2 or the convergence is quadratic. It converges if |f(x).f''(x)| < |f'(x)|2. Also, this method fails if f'(x) = 0.

∧*∧*∧*∧*∧*∧*∧*∧*∧*∧*∧*∧*∧*∧*∧*∧*∧*∧*∧*∧*∧*∧∧*∧*∧*∧*∧

Problem: Write a program in Q-basic to find the root of the function below, by using Newton - Raphson method:

X0 = 3 , E = 0.005 F ( X) = X 2 – 4 SIN( X) ,
*********************************************************************

```
CLS
 READ X0, E
DATA 1,0.0001
DEF FNF (X) = X ^ 2 - 4 * SIN(X)
DEF FNG (X) = 2 * X - 4 * COS(X)
 5 X1 = X0 - (FNF(X0) / FNG(X0))
PRINT X1
IF ABS(X1 - X0) < E THEN 25
 X0 = X1: GOTO 5
25 PRINT "THE ROOT IS:", C
END
```
*********************************************************************

# Iteration Method

In computational mathematics, an iterative method is a mathematical procedure that uses an initial value to generate a sequence of improving approximate solutions for a class of problems, in which the n-th approximation is derived from the previous ones.

\*\*\*\*\*\*\*\*\*\*\*\*\*\*\*\*\*\*\*\*\*\*\*\*\*\*\*\*_____\*\*\*\*\*\*\*\*\*\*\*\*\*\*\*\*\*\*\*\*\*\*\*\*\*\*\*\*

Problem: Write a program in Q-basic to find the root of the function below, by using iteration method:

$X0 = 4$ , $E = 0.001$ $F ( X) = X ^2 - 2 *X - 3$ ,

\*\*\*\*\*\*\*\*\*\*\*\*\*\*\*\*\*\*\*\*\*\*\*\*\*\*\*\*\*\*\*\*\*\*\*\*\*\*\*\*\*\*\*\*\*\*\*\*\*\*\*\*\*\*\*\*\*\*\*\*\*\*\*\*\*\*\*\*\*\*\*\*\*\*

```
CLS
READ X0, E
DATA 4,.001
DEF FNF (X) = SQR(2 * X -3 ) 5 X1 = FNF(X0)
PRINT X1
IF ABS(X1 - X0) < E THEN 25
X0 = X1: GOTO 5
25 PRINT "THE ROOT IS:", X1
END
```

\*\*\*\*\*\*\*\*\*\*\*\*\*\*\*\*\*\*\*\*\*\*\*\*\*\*\*\*\*\*\*\*\*\*\*\*\*\*\*\*\*\*\*\*\*\*\*\*\*\*\*\*\*\*\*\*\*\*\*\*\*\*\*\*\*\*\*\*\*\*\*\*\*\*

Problem: Write a program in Q-basic to find the root of the function below, by using itiken method:

Xo = 3 , e = 0.001 f ( x) = x 2 – x – 2 ,

**********************************************************************

```
CLS
 READ X0, E
DATA 3,.001
DEF FNF (X) = 1 + 2 / X 10 X1 = FNF(X0) X2 = FNF(X1) X3 =
FNF(X2)
 PRINT X0, X1, X2 XX = X2 - ((X2 - X1) ^ 2 / (X2 - 2 * X1 + X0))
 PRINT XX
IF ABS(XX - X0) < E
THEN 25 X0 = XX: GOTO 10
 25 PRINT "THE ROOT IS:"; XX
END
```

**********************************************************************

# Gauss Elimination Method

It is used to solve a system of linear equations. Let's recall the definition of these systems of equations. A system of linear equations is a group of linear equations with various unknown factors. As we know, unknown factors exist in multiple equations. Solving a system involves finding the value for the unknown factors to verify all the equations that make up the system.

Problem: Write a program in Q-basic to solve the system, by using Gauss elimination:
4 x1 − 9 x2 + 2 x3 = 5 2 x1 − 4 x2 + 6 x3 = 3 x1 − x2 + 3x3 = 4

**********************************************************************

```
CLS
 N = 3: M = N + 1
DIM A(N, M), X(N)
FOR I = 1 TO N
 FOR J = 1 TO M
 READ A(I, J)
 DATA 4,-9,2,5,2,-4,6,3,1,-1,3,4
 NEXT J
NEXT I
 FOR K = 1 TO N - 1
FOR I = K + 1 TO N
 B = A(I, K) / A(K, K)
FOR J = 1 TO M
 A(I, J) = A(I, J) - A(K, J) * B
 NEXT J
NEXT I
 NEXT K
 X(N) = A(N, M) / A(N, N)
FOR I = N - 1 TO 1 STEP -1
 S=0 FOR J = N TO I + 1 STEP -1
S = S + A(I, J) * X(J)
NEXT J X(J) = (A(I, M) - S) / A(I, I)
 NEXT I
FOR I = 1 TO N
 PRINT X(I)
NEXT I
```

END
**************************************************************************

Problem: Write a program in Q-basic to solve the system, by using Gauss Jorden method:

x1 + x3 = 1
x1 + x 2 = 1
x 2 + x3 = 1
**************************************************************************

```
CLS
n = 3: m = n + 1
DIM a(n, m), x(n)
FOR i = 1 TO n
FOR j = 1 TO m
 READ a(i, j)
DATA 1,0,1,1,1,1,0,1,0,1,1,1
NEXT j
NEXT i
 FOR k = 1 TO n - 1
FOR i = k + 1 TO n b = a(i, k) / a(k, k)
 FOR j = 1 TO m
 a(i, j) = a(i, j) - a(k, j) * b
NEXT j
 NEXT i
NEXT k
FOR k = n TO n - 1 STEP -1
 FOR i = k - 1 TO 1 STEP -1
 b = a(i, k) / a(k, k)
 FOR j = m TO 1 STEP -1
 a(i, j) = a(i, j) - a(k, j) * b
NEXT j
 NEXT i
NEXT k
FOR i = 1 TO n
x(i) = a(i, m) / a(i, i)
 PRINT x(i)
NEXT i
```

end
\*\*\*\*\*\*\*\*\*\*\*\*\*\*\*\*\*\*\*\*\*\*\*\*\*\*\*\*\*\*\*\*\*\*\*\*\*\*\*\*\*\*\*\*\*\*\*\*\*\*\*\*\*\*\*\*\*\*\*\*\*\*\*\*\*\*\*\*\*\*\*\*\*\*\*\*\*\*\*\*\*\*

Problem: Write a program in Q-basic to solve the system, by using Jaccobi method: $10 x_1 + x_2 + x_3 = 12$ $x_1 + 10 x_2 + x_3 = 12$ $x_1 + x_2 + 10 x_3 = 12$
\*\*\*\*\*\*\*\*\*\*\*\*\*\*\*\*\*\*\*\*\*\*\*\*\*\*\*\*\*\*\*\*\*\*\*\*\*\*\*\*\*\*\*\*\*\*\*\*\*\*\*\*\*\*\*\*\*\*\*\*\*\*\*\*\*\*\*\*\*\*\*\*\*\*\*\*\*\*\*\*\*\*

```
CLS
 READ n, e
DATA 3,0.00001
DIM a(n, n), b(n), x(n), y(n)
FOR i = 1 TO n
 FOR j = 1 TO n
READ a(i, j)
DATA 10,1,1,1,10,1,1,1,10
NEXT j
 NEXT i
 FOR i = 1 TO n
 READ b(i)
 DATA 12,12,12
 NEXT i
FOR i = 1 TO n
y(i) = 0
NEXT i
 5 FOR i = 1 TO n
 s = 0: d = 0
 FOR j = 1 TO n
 IF i = j THEN 7
s = s + a(i, j) * y(j)
7 NEXT j x(i) = (b(i) - s) / a(i, i)
 PRINT x(i) d = d + ABS(x(i) - y(i))
 NEXT i IF d < e THEN 2
FOR i = 1 TO n
y(i) = x(i)
 NEXT i GOTO 5
 2 PRINT
 FOR i = 1 TO n
```

```
 PRINT x(i)
 NEXT i
 END
 ***********************************************************************
```

# Gauss–Seidel Method

In numerical linear algebra, the Gauss–Seidel method, also known as the Liebmann method or the method of successive displacement, is an iterative method used to solve a system of linear equations
In numerical linear algebra, the Gauss–Seidel method, also known as the Liebmann method or the method of successive displacement, is an iterative method used to solve a system of linear equations.

## Description

The Gauss–Seidel method is an iterative technique for solving a square system of n linear equations. Let Ax = b be sqare system of n linear equations. where -

$$A = \begin{bmatrix} a_{11} & a_{12} & \cdots & a_{1n} \\ a_{21} & a_{22} & \cdots & a_{2n} \\ \vdots & \vdots & \ddots & \vdots \\ a_{n1} & a_{n2} & \cdots & a_{nn} \end{bmatrix}, \quad \mathbf{x} = \begin{bmatrix} x_1 \\ x_2 \\ \vdots \\ x_n \end{bmatrix}, \quad \mathbf{b} = \begin{bmatrix} b_1 \\ b_2 \\ \vdots \\ b_n \end{bmatrix}.$$

where A and B are known, and x is unknown. we can use gauss-seidel method to approximate x. the vector x0 denotes our initial gauss for x.

we denote $x^{\wedge}(k)$ as the k-th approximation or iteration of x,and $x^{\wedge}(+1)$ is the next (or $k+1$) iteration of x.

## Matrix-based formula

The solution is obtained iteratively via

$$L_* \mathbf{x}^{(k+1)} = \mathbf{b} - U\mathbf{x}^{(k)},$$

whwere the matrix A is decomposed into a lower triangular component L*, and strictly upper triangular component U . such that A= L* + U. more specially the decomposition of A into L* and U is given by :

$$A = \underbrace{\begin{bmatrix} a_{11} & 0 & \cdots & 0 \\ a_{21} & a_{22} & \cdots & 0 \\ \vdots & \vdots & \ddots & \vdots \\ a_{n1} & a_{n2} & \cdots & a_{nn} \end{bmatrix}}_{L_*} + \underbrace{\begin{bmatrix} 0 & a_{12} & \cdots & a_{1n} \\ 0 & 0 & \cdots & a_{2n} \\ \vdots & \vdots & \ddots & \vdots \\ 0 & 0 & \cdots & 0 \end{bmatrix}}_{U}.$$

## Convergence

The convergence properties of the Gauss–Seidel method are dependent on the matrix A. Namely, the procedure is known to converge if either:

1. A is symmetric positive-definite.
2. A is strictly or irreducibly diagonally dominant.

3. The Gauss–Seidel method sometimes converges even if these conditions are not satisfied.

^*^*^*^*^*^*^*^*^*^*^*^*^*^*^*^*^*^*^*^*^*^*^*^**^*^*^*^*^*^*^

Problem: Write a program in Q-basic to solve the system, by using Gauss Seidel method:

10 x1 + x2 + x3 = 12 x1 + 10 x2 + x3 = 12 x1 + x2 + 10 x3 = 12

*************************************************************************

```
CLS
READ n, e
DATA 3,0.00001
DIM a(n, n), b(n), x(n), y(n)
FOR i = 1 TO n
FOR j = 1 TO n
READ a(i, j)
DATA 10,1,1,1,10,1,1,1,10
NEXT j
NEXT i
FOR i = 1 TO n
READ b(i)
DATA 12,12,12
NEXT i
FOR i = 1 TO n y(i) = 0
NEXT i
5 FOR i = 1 TO n
s1 = 0: s2 = 0
FOR j = 1 TO n
IF i = j THEN 2
IF i < j THEN
s1 = s1 + a(i, j) * y(j)
IF i > j THEN s2 = s2 + a(i, j) * x(j) 2
NEXT j s = s1 + s2 x(i) = (b(i) - s) / a(i, i)
NEXT i d=0
FOR i = 1 TO n
```

```
 d = d + ABS(x(i) - y(i))
NEXT i
 IF d < e THEN 3
FOR i = 1 TO n y(i) = x(i)
 NEXT i

GOTO 5
 3 PRINT
 FOR i = 1 TO n
PRINT x(i)
NEXT i
END
```

**************************************************************************

ΔΔΔ

"if you are self motivated then no one can ever de-motivate you"

## - Poornima Gontiya

✿✿✿✿✿✿✿✿✿**THANK-YOU** ✿✿✿✿✿✿✿✿✿

# ABOUT THE AUTHOR

## Poornima Gontiya

I'm an artist who loves creative things. I have done Msc. in physics and studied the core subjects to enhance my knowledge. blogging, writing quotes is my favorite thing to express from within. meeting new people from different cultures and traditions helps me out to explore the different colors of lives. travelling is the best way to learn and explore the hidden secrets of life. learning new things always excites me to gain knowledge. observing life and imprinting it on my life's canvas and expressing through words are my favorite things to express my gratitude towards the supreme power "the universe".

"Writing is the best way to raise your voice against every injustice but it can only be possible if you hold the power of Education".

# BOOKS BY THIS AUTHOR

## Ask The Universe

This book is based on the universal power and manifestation technique . we all know that there is a power beyond science which works on vibrations. vibrations can be negative or positive this is the full summarized guide to use positive words and affirmations for transforming your life. this book will make you believe that law of attraction does works if you use correct way with right approach.

## Birsa Munda: The Great Warrior

THIS BOOK IS BASED ON THE GREAT WARRIOR, GOD BIRSA MUNDA. THIS BOOK IS BASED ON ALL THE MOVEMENTS AND REBELLIONS WHOSE IMPRINTS STILL SURVIVE ON THE GOLDEN PAGES OF INDIAN HISTORY. BIRSA WAS A SOCIAL REFORMER, GUIDE, AND CHRIST FOR THE BIRAPANTHIES (THE FOLLOWER OF BIRSA ) IT IS NOT POSSIBLE TO DESCRIBE THE LIFE OF BIRSA . I AM SURE ABOUT THAT BY READING THIS BOOK MY READERS CAN EASILY GET THE IDEAS OF BIRSA MUNDA .

## The Environmental Physics

We all know that without science the environment is like a closed door. especially physics helps us to open the door to the mysterious world of the environment. Here we can't consider an environment of just one field. The whole universe is a part of physics or we can say that physics is the key to the unlocked world of space, technologies, the internal earth, the giant web of cloud computing and networking, digital communication, demodulation techniques, and this list goes on and on. This book is all about the vast knowledge of the consanguinity of physics and environment and also the never-ending scope in this field as a carrier.

## The Marriage Proposal: The Story Of The Civil Services Aspirant

This is the story of a civil servant who confronts the reality of life when she got in trouble along with her friends and solve the mystery of a crime which was happened 15 years back, read this story to explore this amazing life of an aspirant who turned into a spy .

## My Inner Thoughts: A Conversation With My Soul

The problem in this journey of life is endless. You can't ignore your wellness and a healthy lifestyle. Day to day busy schedules makes life more hectic and unbearable. Some people are introvert and some are extrovert both have different perspective of solving problems. Some say it clearly some believe to be conserved. But here my question is that if you will not express what you are really feeling and from what you are going through then how the other people will able to solve your problem. This book is exactly the second person as a mirror which is a reflection your inner emotions and unuttered words. It is the healing tablet which will teach you what should you do to solve your problems by yourself. So read this book. Help yourself and live a better and a healthy life.

www.ingramcontent.com/pod-product-compliance
Lightning Source LLC
Chambersburg PA
CBHW070333220526
45467CB00001B/127